Introduction to Representation

Grades PreK–2

Other Books in The Math Process Standards Series

Introduction to Problem Solving: Grades PreK–2 (O'Connell)
Introduction to Reasoning and Proof: Grades PreK–2
(Schultz-Ferrell, Hammond, and Robles)
Introduction to Communication: Grades PreK–2 (O'Connell and O'Connor)
Introduction to Connections: Grades PreK–2 (Bamberger and Oberdorf)

For information on the 3–5 grades and 6–8 grades series see the Heinemann website, www.heinemann.com.

Introduction to Representation

Grades PreK–2

Kimberly S. Witeck
Bonnie H. Ennis

The Math Process Standards Series
Susan O'Connell, Series Editor

HEINEMANN
Portsmouth, NH

Heinemann
A division of Reed Elsevier Inc.
361 Hanover Street
Portsmouth, NH 03801–3912
www.heinemann.com

Offices and agents throughout the world

The authors and publisher wish to thank those who have generously given permission to reprint borrowed material:

Excerpts from *Principles and Standards for School Mathematics*. Copyright © 2000 by the National Council of Teachers of Mathematics. Reprinted with permission. All rights reserved.

Library of Congress Cataloging-in-Publication Data
Witeck, Kimberly S.
    Introduction to representation : grades pre K–2 / Kimberly S. Witeck, Bonnie H. Ennis.
        p. cm. — (The math process standards series)
    Includes bibliographical references.
    ISBN 978-0-325-01149-3 (alk. paper)
    1. Mathematics—Study and teaching (Preschool)—Standards.
 2. Mathematics—Study and teaching (Preschool)—Activity programs.
 3. Mathematics—Study and teaching (Early childhood)—Standards.
 4. Mathematics—Study and teaching (Early childhood)—Activity programs.
 I. Ennis, Bonnie H.   II. Title.
    QA135.6.W584 2007
    372.7—dc22   2007016194

Editor: Emily Michie Birch
Production coordinator: Elizabeth Valway
Production service: Matrix Productions Inc.
Cover design: Night & Day Design
Cover photography: Lauren Robertson
Composition: Publishers' Design and Production Services, Inc.
CD production: Nicole Russell and Marla Berry
Manufacturing: Jamie Carter

Printed in the United States of America on acid-free paper
11   10   09   08   07   ML   1   2   3   4   5

To Mom and Dad, my first teachers.

—KSW

To Ann

—BHE

On the CD-ROM

In order to be effective mathematicians, students need to develop understanding of critical math content. They need to understand number and operations, algebra, measurement, geometry, and data analysis and probability. Through continued study of these content domains, students gain a comprehensive understanding of mathematics as a subject with varied and interconnected concepts. As math teachers, we attempt to provide students with exposure to, exploration in, and reflection about the many skills and concepts that make up the study of mathematics.

Even with a deep understanding of math content, however, students may lack important skills that can assist them in their development as effective mathematicians. Along with content knowledge, students need an understanding of the processes used by mathematicians. They must learn to problem solve, communicate their ideas, reason through math situations, prove their conjectures, make connections between and among math concepts, and represent their mathematical thinking. Development of content alone does not provide students with the means to explore, express, or apply that content. As we strive to develop effective mathematicians, we are challenged to develop both students' content understanding and process skills.

The National Council of Teachers of Mathematics (2000) has outlined critical content and process standards in its *Principles and Standards for School Mathematics* document. These standards have become the roadmap for the development of textbooks, curriculum materials, and student assessments. These standards have provided a framework for thinking about what needs to be taught in math classrooms and how various skills and concepts can be blended together to create a seamless math curriculum. The first five standards outline content standards and expectations related to number and operations, algebra, geometry, measurement, and data analysis and probability. The second five standards outline the process goals of problem solving, reasoning and proof, communication, connections, and representations. A strong understanding of these standards empowers teachers to identify and select activities within their curricula to produce powerful learning. The standards provide a vision for what teachers hope their students will achieve.

This book is a part of a vital series designed to assist teachers in understanding the NCTM Process Standards and the ways in which they impact and guide student learning. An additional goal of this series is to provide practical ideas to support teachers as they ensure that the acquisition of process skills has a critical place in their math instruction. Through this series, teachers will gain an understanding of each process standard as well as gather ideas for bringing that standard to life within their math classrooms. It offers practical ideas for lesson development, implementation, and assessment that work with any curriculum. Each book in the series focuses on a critical process skill in a highlighted grade band and all books are designed to encourage reflection about teaching and learning. The series also highlights the interconnected nature of the process and content standards by showing correlations between them and showcasing activities that address multiple standards.

Students who develop an understanding of content skills and cultivate the process skills that allow them to apply that content understanding become effective mathematicians. Our goal as teachers is to support and guide students as they develop both their content knowledge and their process skills, so they are able to continue to expand and refine their understanding of mathematics. This series is a guide for math educators who aspire to teach students more than math content. It is a guide to assist teachers in understanding and teaching the critical processes through which students learn and make sense of mathematics.

Susan O'Connell
Series Editor

We would like to thank many people for their support, expertise, guidance, and encouragement during this project. First, thank you to Sue O'Connell for encouraging us to take on this project, for your patient support in reading our work, and for helping to give us a jump start when we needed it. And to Emily Birch, Executive Editor for Math and Science at Heinemann, thanks for always being available to give feedback, support, and encouragement.

From Kimberly Witeck

To the community of teachers and students at Braddock Elementary in Annandale, Virginia, thank you for providing invaluable feedback, support, and your expertise. Thanks especially to Cynthia Botzin, principal at Braddock, for being a model leader for all in the field of education and for allowing me to work with students at the school to gather data and work samples for the book; Judy Hall, Title I math teacher and coach, for her expertise, feedback on particular chapters, and moral support; Gwenanne Salkind, Title I Assistant Program Supervisor, for her expertise and guidance in clarifying concepts in the book; and Aaron Davis, Christine Fisher, Erin Channell, Claudia Trace, Emilie Wheat, Sheryl Rauer, and Becca Glassner, teachers at Braddock, for allowing me to work with their students.

The following students were a pleasure to work with and contributed work samples or allowed their photographs to be included in the book: Ali Bascope, Zoe Bates, Isabella Burt, Matthew Cook, Rebecca D., Adriana Diaz, Cassidy Gillis, Melanie Gomez, Willie Hincapie, Jose Alberto Jaldin, Jenny Jang, Celine Jeong, Nithya John, Jeena Kim, Khoshnaw, Ryan McKean, Randy Medina, Jalani Rice, Rai Rocca-Aragones, Jessica Smith, Rachel Soon, Kaylah Strother, Michaela Valdivia Cassol, and Jumana Younes.

Finally, I could not have completed this project without the unwavering support of my husband, Chris, my parents, Skip and Jackie Sterling, and my beautiful children,

Aidan and Caroline, who showed patience beyond their years while I finished this project.

From Bonnie Ennis

To the students, teachers, and administrators of the Wicomico County Public Schools, Salisbury, Maryland, thank you for your advice, support, and expertise throughout the years. A special thank-you to the math professional development coaches of Wicomico County, who continue to amaze me on a daily basis with their creativity, enthusiasm, and willingness to do everything we ask in support of the teachers of our district. It is a pleasure to work with such wonderful professionals.

To the students and staff of Charles H. Chipman Elementary School and Fruitland Primary, thank you for your willingness to provide such wonderful material. To Sue Gebhart, Debbie Dashiell, Stephanie Post-Brinsfield, Cindy Becker, Jackie Lemon, Pat McGowan, Diana Churchman, Michael Wilson, and Peggy Elwood for their expert contributions, advice, and time. The following students were a pleasure to work with and contributed work samples or allowed their photographs to be included in the book: Sean Clendenin, Robert Lane, Christopher Sajadi, Georgia Olivis, Luke Livingston, R. J. Howatt III, Sammy Perez, Ian Wilson, Christopher Taylor, Jessica Dameus, Devin Phillips, Ryan Davey, Ashley Amey, and Benjamin Urban.

Problem-Solving Standard

Instructional programs from prekindergarten through grade 12 should enable all students to—

- build new mathematical knowledge through problem solving;

- solve problems that arise in mathematics and in other contexts;

- apply and adapt a variety of appropriate strategies to solve problems;

- monitor and reflect on the process of mathematical problem solving.

Reasoning and Proof Standard

Instructional programs from prekindergarten through grade 12 should enable all students to—

- recognize reasoning and proof as fundamental aspects of mathematics;

- make and investigate mathematical conjectures;

- develop and evaluate mathematical arguments and proofs;

- select and use various types of reasoning and methods of proof.

---

*Standards are listed with the permission of the National Council of Teachers of Mathematics (NCTM). NCTM does not endorse the content or validity of these alignments.

Communication Standard

Instructional programs from prekindergarten through grade 12 should enable all students to—

- organize and consolidate their mathematical thinking through communication;

- communicate their mathematical thinking coherently and clearly to peers, teachers, and others;

- analyze and evaluate the mathematical thinking and strategies of others;

- use the language of mathematics to express mathematical ideas precisely.

Connections Standard

Instructional programs from prekindergarten through grade 12 should enable all students to—

- recognize and use connections among mathematical ideas;

- understand how mathematical ideas interconnect and build on one another to produce a coherent whole;

- recognize and apply mathematics in contexts outside of mathematics.

Representation Standard

Instructional programs from prekindergarten through grade 12 should enable all students to—

- create and use representations to organize, record, and communicate mathematical ideas;

- select, apply, and translate among mathematical representations to solve problems;

- use representations to model and interpret physical, social, and mathematical phenomena.

NCTM Content Standards and Expectations for Grades PreK–2

NUMBER AND OPERATIONS

	Expectations
Instructional programs from prekindergarten through grade 12 should enable all students to—	**In prekindergarten through 2nd grade all students should—**
Understand numbers, ways of representing numbers, relationships among numbers, and number systems	• count with understanding and recognize "how many" in sets of objects; • use multiple models to develop initial understandings of place value and the base-ten number system; • develop understanding of the relative position and magnitude of whole numbers and of ordinal and cardinal numbers and their connections; • develop a sense of whole numbers and represent and use them in flexible ways, including relating, composing, and decomposing numbers; • connect number words and numerals to the quantities they represent, using various physical models and representations; • understand and represent commonly used fractions, such as 1/4, 1/3, and 1/2.
Understand meanings of operations and how they relate to one another	• understand various meanings of addition and subtraction of whole numbers and the relationship between the two operations; • understand the effects of adding and subtracting whole numbers; • understand situations that entail multiplication and division, such as equal groupings of objects and sharing equally.
Compute fluently and make reasonable estimates	• develop and use strategies for whole-number computations, with a focus on addition and subtraction;

	Expectations
Instructional programs from prekindergarten through grade 12 should enable all students to—	**In prekindergarten through 2nd grade all students should—**
	• develop fluency with basic number combinations for addition and subtraction; • use a variety of methods and tools to compute, including objects, mental computation, estimation, paper and pencil, and calculators.

ALGEBRA

	Expectations
Instructional programs from prekindergarten through grade 12 should enable all students to—	**In prekindergarten through 2nd grade all students should—**
Understand patterns, relations, and functions	• sort, classify, and order objects by size, number, and other properties; • recognize, describe, and extend patterns such as sequences of sounds and shapes or simple numeric patterns and translate from one representation to another; • analyze how both repeating and growing patterns are generated.
Represent and analyze mathematical situations and structures using algebraic symbols	• illustrate general principles and properties of operations, such as commutativity, using specific numbers; • use concrete, pictorial, and verbal representations to develop an understanding of invented and conventional symbolic notations.
Use mathematical models to represent and understand quantitative relationships	• model situations that involve the addition and subtraction of whole numbers, using objects, pictures, and symbols.
Analyze change in various contexts	• describe qualitative change, such as a student's growing taller; • describe quantitative change, such as a student's growing two inches in one year.

GEOMETRY

	Expectations
Instructional programs from prekindergarten through grade 12 should enable all students to—	**In prekindergarten through 2nd grade all students should—**
Analyze characteristics and properties of two- and three-dimensional geometric shapes and develop mathematical arguments about geometric relationships	• recognize, name, build, draw, compare, and sort two- and three-dimensional shapes; • describe attributes and parts of two- and three-dimensional shapes; • investigate and predict the results of putting together and taking apart two- and three-dimensional shapes.
Specify locations and describe spatial relationships using coordinate geometry and other representational systems	• describe, name, and interpret relative positions in space and apply ideas about relative position; • describe, name, and interpret direction and distance in navigating space and apply ideas about direction and distance; • find and name locations with simple relationships such as "near to" and in coordinate systems such as maps.
Apply transformations and use symmetry to analyze mathematical situations	• recognize and apply slides, flips, and turns; • recognize and create shapes that have symmetry.
Use visualization, spatial reasoning, and geometric modeling to solve problems	• create mental images of geometric shapes using spatial memory and spatial visualization; • recognize and represent shapes from different perspectives; • relate ideas in geometry to ideas in number and measurement; • recognize geometric shapes and structures in the environment and specify their location.

MEASUREMENT

	Expectations
Instructional programs from prekindergarten through grade 12 should enable all students to—	**In prekindergarten through 2nd grade all students should—**
Understand measurable attributes of objects and the units, systems, and processes of measurement	• recognize the attributes of length, volume, weight, area, and time; • compare and order objects according to these attributes; • understand how to measure using nonstandard and standard units; • select an appropriate unit and tool for the attribute being measured.
Apply appropriate techniques, tools, and formulas to determine measurements	• measure with multiple copies of units of the same size, such as paper clips laid end to end; • use repetition of a single unit to measure something larger than the unit, for instance, measuring the length of a room with a single meterstick; • use tools to measure; • develop common referents for measures to make comparisons and estimates.

DATA ANALYSIS AND PROBABILITY

	Expectations
Instructional programs from prekindergarten through grade 12 should enable all students to—	**In prekindergarten through 2nd grade all students should—**
Formulate questions that can be addressed with data and collect, organize, and display relevant data to answer them	• pose questions and gather data about themselves and their surroundings; • sort and classify objects according to their attributes and organize data about the objects; • represent data using concrete objects, pictures, and graphs.
Select and use appropriate statistical methods to analyze data	• describe parts of the data and the set of data as a whole to determine what the data show.
Develop and evaluate inferences and predictions that are based on data	• discuss events related to students' experiences as likely or unlikely.
Understand and apply basic concepts of probability	

Introduction to Representation

The Representation Standard

The ways in which mathematical ideas are represented is fundamental to how people can understand and use those ideas.

—National Council of Teachers of Mathematics,
Principles and Standards for School Mathematics

What Are Representations?

Doesn't it sometimes seem as if students in primary math classes should all come equipped with hard hats and tool belts instead of just paper and pencils! At this early stage it is all about constructing important understandings about mathematical concepts and connecting those understandings, not just to one another but to the world around them. It isn't about a single right answer to a missing addend problem; it isn't merely about circling the right picture; it isn't even about doing a whole page of addition or subtraction problems. Practice to improve fluency in computation is certainly important, as noted by NCTM's Focal Points, but math at this level must include opportunities that are much richer. How is it that we can get at early student thinking, and what types of math representations can we model to promote students' communication of that thinking? It is important to note that we can't ask students to represent something that they haven't yet learned. Are students at this stage even capable of somehow putting on paper the processes and thinking they have as they work through a number pattern or pattern of shapes? What does it truly mean to ask students to represent their mathematical thinking, and how can we support, model for, and encourage students to put on paper their interpretations of the mathematical models that helped them make those crucial connections between the concrete and the abstract?

Representing their solutions using pictures, diagrams, concrete models, numbers, and words is one of the means by which students can communicate to others their mathematical thinking and at the same time clarify in their own mind what meaning lies in the mathematics. Admittedly, at the primary level student-produced representations may be limited in scope and sophistication, but students should still be encouraged to create their own representations when appropriate. At the same time they need to be provided with multiple opportunities to see and experience representations that have already been created. As their ability to recognize multiple representations improves, so will their ability to produce multiple representations that communicate their own understandings. The goal is to increase students' ability to construct meaning and at the same time improve their number sense. As teachers, we need to look for a variety of pictures, words, and concrete models that help our students construct meaning.

Manipulatives and concrete models provide students with important visuals that help to model the mathematics at hand, but they are just that—models. It is up to us as teachers to help students make the connections between the models and the mathematical concepts. Only by making those connections will students truly understand and internalize the math. Once those connections have been made, students can begin representing their own thinking in words, pictures, symbols, and diagrams and, later on, apply their knowledge to more complex problem-solving situations. Representations take many forms: an algorithm that can be used to represent a problem situation, a graph that represents data collected in the classroom, an array that shows a subtraction process, or diagrams that illustrate. Numbers, pictures, diagrams, equations, graphs, and models are all forms of mathematical representations. In the past, standard representations were simply taught to students, but teachers are now recognizing the power of alternative representations as tools through which students can explore and enhance their mathematical thinking.

The National Council of Teachers of Mathematics' *Principles and Standards for School Mathematics* (2000) describes representations as fundamental to understanding and applying mathematics, and it makes three recommendations for using them in the mathematics classroom:

1. teachers should employ "representations to model and interpret physical, social, and mathematical phenomena" (NCTM 2000, 70);

2. students should be familiar with and comprehend various representations that can be used to describe phenomena; and

3. students should use mathematical representations to organize their thinking and reflect on numerical or geometric information.

Representations, instead of being taught to students, are valuable ways in which students can explore their own math thinking. Finding ways to represent their ideas pushes students to think more deeply about those ideas as they determine ways to communicate them to others. Representations give us insight into our students' understandings by providing students with a way of working through their thought processes. When students use base ten blocks to model addition or subtraction problems, draw circles or squares, or create a pictograph to organize and then analyze data, they are using various forms of representation to demonstrate their mathematical thinking. It is important that we give students many opportunities to represent their thinking and guide them to become proficient in representation. As they become more comfortable creating representations of their ideas, their mathematical thinking will greatly expand, as will their ability to communicate about that thinking.

Representation is both a process and a product by which students are able to explore and sort out mathematical concepts as well as communicate mathematically with their peers. Because representation is both a process and a product, students need many and varied opportunities to explore and sort mathematical concepts and to communicate these concepts to their peers. They need opportunities that will ultimately guide them toward more conventional forms of representation, facilitating their mathematical thinking and deepening their understanding. By enabling students to use a wide variety of representations, we are helping them to assemble a repertoire of tools from which to draw when exploring mathematical concepts.

What Is the Representation Standard?

Principles and Standards for School Mathematics (NCTM 2000) outlines standards for both math content and math processes. The content standards help us identify key math content that is critical to students' understanding of mathematics, and the process standards help us identify those processes through which students learn and apply math content. Representation is a critical math process that supports students in their learning of math and their ability to express that learning.

In NCTM's original standards document, *Curriculum and Evaluation Standards for School Mathematics* (1989), representation was included as a part of the communication standard, one of the four process standards in the original document. In the 2000 document, five process standards are outlined, with communication and representation individually addressed. NCTM now treats representation as its own process standard in order to address the broad scope of representation and its importance in learning mathematics. It has been recognized that the ability to represent ideas is fundamental to the study of mathematics.

In *Principles and Standards for School Mathematics*, NCTM recommends that instructional programs from prekindergarten through grade 12 should enable all students to—

- create and use representations to organize, record, and communicate mathematical ideas;

- select, apply, and translate among mathematical representations to solve problems; and

- use representations to model and interpret physical, social, and mathematical phenomena.

The abilities to create representations to illustrate ideas, communicate thinking through representations, determine which representation would best fit a concept or idea, and use representation to model math situations are all critical components of this standard.

How Can Representation Support Student Learning?

Representation is both about helping students find their own ways to represent math ideas and about helping them understand conventional representations of math ideas (e.g., whole numbers, place value, fact families, patterns, charts, graphs, and diagrams). Students should be encouraged to represent their ideas and understandings in ways that make sense to them. Those representations provide key information for a teacher trying to determine where a student falls on the learning continuum.

Consider the following problem given to kindergarten, first and second grade students, each with a very different solution.

Use the numbers 14, 9, and 5 to draw a story problem.

No other conditions were set, and the students were encouraged to express their ideas using any operation or setting that made sense to them. By providing students with open-ended problems such as this, a teacher is able to gain more insight into the thinking of a student as his or her story unfolds. Asher, a kindergarten student, completed his story problem by first drawing an illustration of fourteen cars (Figure I–1). Since fourteen is the first number, that isn't an unusual place for a kindergarten student to start. The interesting part of his work is that he skipped over the nine and used the five as the second part and crossed through five cars leaving nine. Once he had his problem drawn, Asher wrote a descriptive sentence that matched his drawing completely. Even though Asher didn't show a connection to the algorithm, his drawing and his sentence show an understanding, even at this early age, of the process of subtraction. No doubt, with questioning, Asher would be able to supply the rest.

Ryan, a first-grade student, chose to use the three numbers to create an addition problem, combining the two smaller numbers to equal the third. His realistic representation of the bugs shows his ability to connect the math to a real-world situation, and he supported his picture with the appropriate numbers (Figure I–2). His written description of the situation provided information on what he was thinking as he completed the task. At this point Ryan has demonstrated that he has a sense of what it means to join two groups together to make one. This process of joining numbers is one of the very basic structures in early addition. With some further questioning, Ryan was able to orally communicate additional solutions using the three numbers.

Devin, a second-grade student, had a somewhat different approach to the same problem. Instead of using a realistic drawing, he chose to use an iconic representation (circles) for his solution. He extended the numbers to include all of the combinations possible for this fact family by showing all of the possible combinations of addition

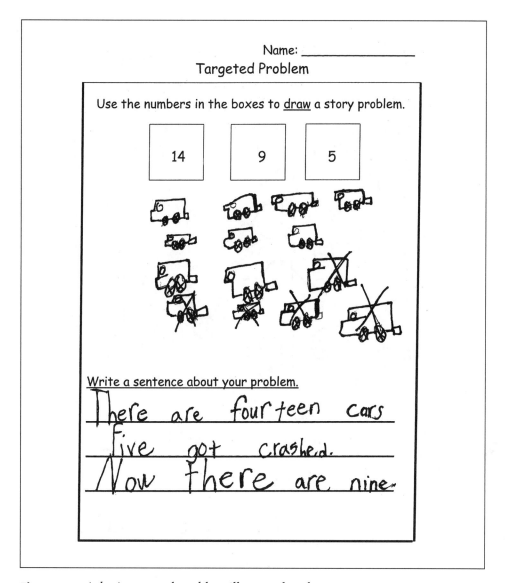

Name: _____
Targeted Problem

Use the numbers in the boxes to <u>draw</u> a story problem.

| 14 | 9 | 5 |

<u>Write a sentence about your problem.</u>

There are fourteen cars
Five got crashed.
Now there are nine.

Figure I–1 *Asher's targeted problem illustrated with cars.*

and subtraction problems (Figure I–3). While his pictorial representation and written communication support only one of the problems, he obviously has a sense of the relationship these numbers have to one another, and he was able to communicate that relationship numerically.

Are these different representations examples that you might expect from primary students? Does the thinking represented in any of them provide any clues to the level of understanding and conceptualization they have of the number facts or the numbers themselves, and has the representation itself helped to support their learning? In this case, Devin certainly seems to have an understanding of how the numbers are related, and he demonstrated that understanding by including the four possible combinations. Ryan also seems to have a clear picture of the relationship of the three numbers, and the fact that he chose to start with nine instead of fourteen is significant. Most students will start their problems with the first number they are given. Ryan, however, chose to

Name: _____

Targeted Problem

Use the numbers in the boxes to <u>draw</u> a story problem.

| 14 | 9 | 5 |

<u>Write a sentence about your problem.</u>

4 bugs under grond
5 more come
in then   there

Was 14 bugs in all

Figure 1-2 *Ryan's targeted problem illustrated with bugs.*

start with the second number. Allowing time for oral communication in a problem such as this, when specific written communication may not be possible, is an important step in getting at a student's thinking. Although many representations are conventional, not all students will show their thinking in conventional ways. It is important that we allow them to work through their thinking in ways that make sense to them and then guide them toward more conventional representations to assist them in better understanding mathematics, as well as to enable others to understand their thought processes.

In this book you will see many examples of ways in which you can provide students with opportunities to represent their thinking and of how to enable them to use those representations in meaningful ways. The process of representation, which is the act of putting one's ideas into words, pictures, numbers, or symbols, is as important as the product: the actual representation of those ideas. We must provide students with many opportunities and ongoing support as they attempt to represent their own ideas and as they explore standard ways to represent math ideas.

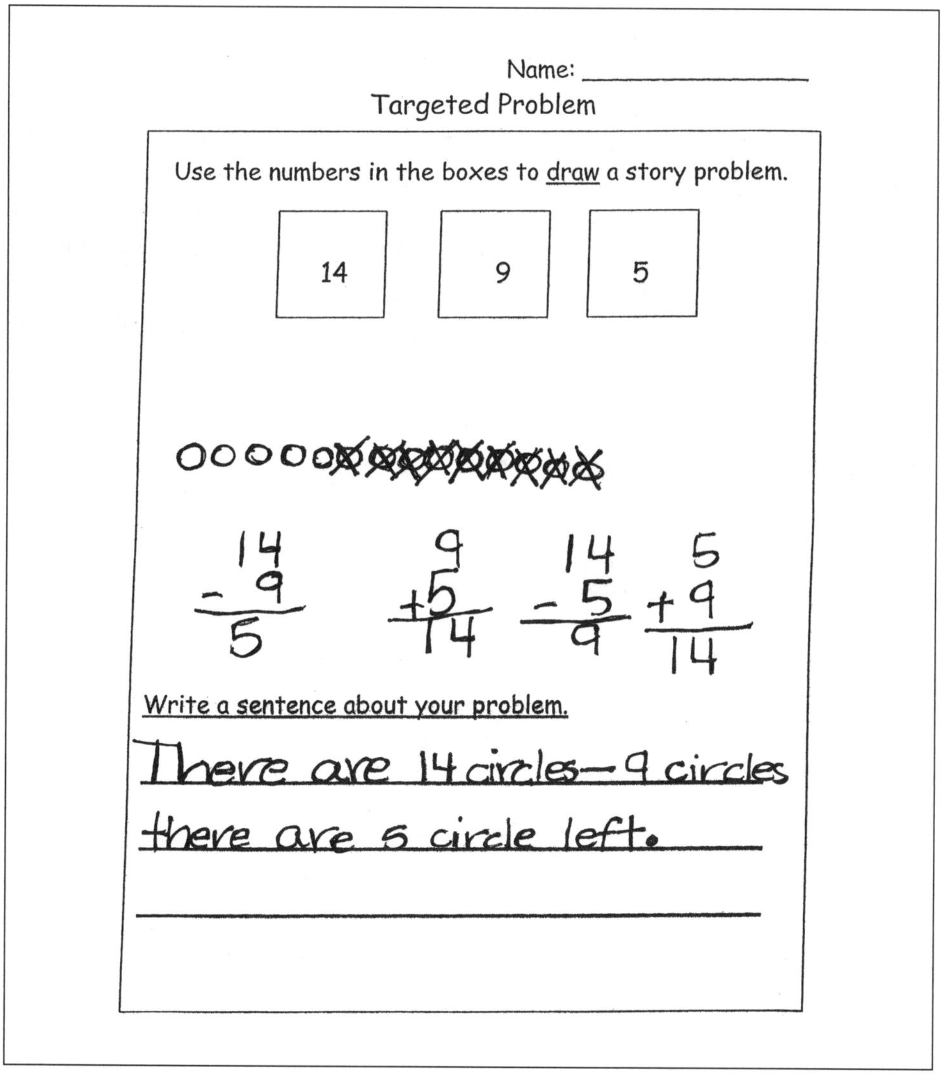

Figure I–3 *Devin's targeted problem using iconic representation.*

In addition to providing students with many opportunities to represent their thinking, we must expose them to a variety of representations. When teaching the concept of subtraction with regrouping, Mr. Wilson chose to provide his students with base ten blocks that they could manipulate to illustrate the need for regrouping. At the same time, he modeled the processes of regrouping using interactive white board technology. As he gives his students a problem to work through, they can see if their manipulatives mirror the ones Mr. Wilson is using. It is important, too, to include in our instruction other ways of representing subtraction, such as pictures, numbers, and words. In addition, as students' mathematical thinking matures, they learn to choose more alternate ways of representing their ideas and information. For example, when faced with a set of data, a second-grade student might need to decide how to graphically represent the information on a pictograph. A first-grade student being asked to demonstrate understanding of the difference between odd and even numbers may need to use tiles or ten frames to represent the differences. By encouraging children to use multiple representations, we help them build a repertoire from which to choose strategies for solving mathematical problems.

Finally, students should use representations to model real-world phenomena. One student might record the daily temperature in her town each day for a week and then represent the data in a table, whereas a student interested in learning which lunch choice is most popular in the school cafeteria might collect data from classmates and then use a real graph to represent these findings to peers, teachers, and the principal. Providing students with opportunities to model different phenomena in the world around them leads to a better understanding of that world and to the mathematical relationships within it.

Does Your Classroom Look Like a Math Classroom?

Does your classroom speak math, and would someone be able to recognize it as a classroom that places an emphasis on math talk? Many of us have worked hard to have colorful wall displays and bulletin boards made from commercially produced cutouts, but what may be missing is a classroom that clearly says, "This is a math classroom, and math is spoken here." Having a room that clearly demonstrates the importance of sharing students' mathematical ideas and work goes a long way toward creating a culture that encourages student discourse in the area of mathematics. As teachers, we want to be certain students realize that their math writing and drawings are the most important part of what goes on in that classroom on a daily basis.

Building important vocabulary is critical at this point. As teachers, we can go from merely asking students to define math concepts using the glossary in the back of their text to having them write the definitions in their own words, representing each concept using an illustration of their choice, and finally adding a real-life application that is appropriate for the concept. Moving the class from copying dictionary definitions or repeating a given definition to representing concepts in multiple forms is not an easy process. Modeling the process in the beginning is essential, and as students begin to feel more comfortable with this new way of representing the math, they will look forward to creating their own representations, which for them brings real meaning to mathematics. Each week students can help generate a list of two to three terms discussed during the week or terms that may have come up during math lessons. Students can then be encouraged to discuss these words in small groups and plan how they think the concepts could best be represented. Yes, students at this level can learn from one another in a small group setting. By working cooperatively on their representations, students will begin to engage more and more in math conversations, which will help other students clarify concepts that may still be somewhat fuzzy.

At the same time, students may begin to look for more and more ways to demonstrate the real-life applications of the math for their own representations. A wonderful added benefit to this process might become evident at parent conferences. Parents may begin sharing with you ways in which their child is sharing the vocabulary at home. Imagine parents being asked by their child to look at work for examples of math concepts or examples in a newspaper or on the Internet. This home–school connection can be an unexpected bonus of the process and a very welcome communication tool that helps parents keep up to date on topics covered during the week. You may also find that by challenging the students to find the real-life applications, you now have instant wall displays that became sources of conversation around mathematics. There is no doubt about what is valued in your classroom.

Creating a Classroom Environment That Encourages Multiple Student Representations

Teachers can facilitate the process of student representations by creating a classroom that encourages students to represent their math thinking in a variety of ways. One way to encourage a climate of student representation is to provide students with the tools they need to create those representations. Baskets of markers, crayons, and colored pencils to which students have easy access will go a long way toward getting students motivated to express their ideas. Because most students in the beginning see representations as drawings, they may be more inclined to create those drawings if they have drawing tools. It would be great if every classroom had unlimited supplies of easel pads so that students could share their representations for the whole class to see, but we all know that isn't the case. One possible solution is to have bulletin boards covered with brown wrapping paper, or any other solid-colored paper, and allow students to draw their representations directly on the board.

It is also important that students have an opportunity to share their interpretations of the mathematics with those around them and discuss how their representations help them to understand and illustrate the concepts. A room that encourages oral communication and cooperative work either in small groups or in pairs is ideal. When students are able not only to discuss the mathematics with their peers but to listen to them explain their thinking, they are more likely to bring their own meaning to the concepts at hand.

CLASSROOM-TESTED TIP

As students are working on representing their math ideas, consider putting four desks together and placing a precut piece of bathroom tile board (from your local building supply store) on top of the four desks, creating an instant work space. The tile board (made of melamine) should have the same dimensions as the four desks combined. Any manipulatives students may be using will not fall through the cracks, and more important, with a dry-erase marker, students can create their representations right on the table before they put their finished copy on paper. You can do this for pairs of student desks as well. Students working on the tile board can all do the problem in their own way and then share at their table. This also makes a great "gallery walk": students can get up and walk around the room, looking at all of the other solutions and representations of the problem.

A note of warning: smooth the edges of the tile board (using a router or sandpaper) prior to use to eliminate sharp edges and corners, and if the boards are heavy, help students put them on top of their desks.

How Can the Use of Representations Help All Populations?

Classrooms today are becoming increasingly diverse. With added ELL (English language learner) populations as well as the increasingly inclusive nature of all classrooms, it is more important than ever to meet the needs of a wide range of student abilities. At the same time, teachers are becoming more cognizant of the research associated with learning styles, and finding ways to reach those learners is crucial. Teachers who encourage students to represent their mathematical thinking in a variety of ways can help meet the needs of those students who may have difficulty explaining or writing down their thinking in words. Students needing alternate ways of expressing their thinking oftentimes find that pictorial representations open a much-needed path for communication. For example, an ELL student will find it much easier to solve a problem that is presented to him pictorially than written out. Likewise, a teacher is much more likely to see a student's thinking when the steps in her solution are either drawn out or written in numeric fashion. The same holds true for special education students working in an inclusive classroom. When the entire class is involved in looking at the math through mathematical models and being encouraged to represent their answers in like fashion, all students feel included and do not feel that they are being singled out for alternate instruction. The key is for all students to feel comfortable with this process and to feel equal in their ability to understand and communicate about mathematics. When asked to "explain their answer" and "show their work," students need to understand that there are a number of ways in which they can do so.

CLASSROOM-TESTED TIP

As students become more comfortable sharing their ideas with others, it is important that all students have an opportunity to participate in an equal fashion. For that reason, equity sticks are a useful tool in any classroom. From a craft department, purchase craft sticks at the beginning of the year and write each student's name on one of the sticks. As you work through a lesson and question the students, reach into the container, pull out an equity stick, and call on the student whose name is written on the stick.

A word of caution in using the sticks: If you have a reluctant learner or a shy student who may not want to answer out loud for fear of being wrong, work out a signal ahead of time so the student can communicate whether or not he or she wants to answer prior to you calling on this student. If you see this signal and know the student feels comfortable enough to answer out loud, then no matter whose name is on the stick you pulled out of the cup, you can call on your reluctant learner. As an added bonus, equity sticks are a great way to help teachers learn students' names at the beginning of the year.

Considerations in Lesson Planning

Ongoing attention to lesson design also helps to create an environment in which students feel comfortable representing their math ideas with pictures, tables, numbers, or manipulatives. Planning lessons that routinely include higher-order questioning, cooperative group work, and class discussions set the stage for productive representation. Using manipulatives, posing problems, and reading math-related literature each provide a stimulus for representing math ideas. A balance of whole-group activities, small teacher-led groups, cooperative groups, partner work, and independent tasks provides varied opportunities for students to develop their representation skills.

In planning lessons, it is important to allow enough time for students to explore math ideas and ways to represent those ideas. Asking follow-up questions that uncover students' reasoning or procedures is vital. Posing fewer tasks but allocating time to discuss ideas and solutions builds students' reasoning and problem-solving skills. Structuring assignments with fewer rote tasks and more reasoning helps balance students' skill development. To ensure that students are not hurried, allow enough time for them to share ideas with others prior to beginning an independent task or spend a few minutes modeling representations prior to assigning an independent task.

Creating an environment that promotes communication is about modifying our expectations from quiet students to verbal students and from correct answers to reflective thinking. It is about developing a community of learners who respect each other's ideas, whether right or wrong, and who work to support each other in building math understanding.

How This Book Will Help You

This book is designed to help you better understand the representation process standard and its significance. Although the book is specifically designed for teachers in prekindergarten through grade 2 and correlates with math content generally taught at those levels, teachers at other grade levels may find strategies and activity ideas that can be used with their students as well. In each section the standards are explained and illustrated through a variety of student work samples, practical ideas are shared for helping students develop their skills in representing mathematical information, and tools to assist you in assessing students' representations are presented.

In Chapter 1, "How Representations Support Learning," a variety of strategies are presented that illustrate the importance of providing students with opportunities to create representations that make math meaningful to them. The chapter also offers some suggested interpretations teachers might make about the levels of student understanding just from looking at student representations. In addition, you will find some practical applications for getting at student representations for various strands of mathematics such as the use of pictorial representations in a variety of problem-solving situations and at various levels of cognitive demand (Figure I–4). Logic problems and their significance in helping students organize solutions in a systematic way are discussed.

Figure I–4 *How many snowmen tall are you?*

Chapter 2, "Using Manipulatives to Model and Illustrate Key Math Concepts," takes a closer look at how the use of manipulatives can guide students as they develop their own representations for the math at hand. Manipulatives are a staple in all math classes. Whether these tools are store-bought or teacher created, the research is clear on their importance. Whether it is in geometry or number computation, manipulatives can provide students with a model that will help them internalize a concept and then enable them to create their own model and interpretation of the math concept. This chapter also provides classroom examples of how the connection between the concrete manipulative and the student representation can be used to build student understanding.

Chapter 3, "Using Pictures and Diagrams to Represent Mathematical Thinking," takes you through some of the possible ways to get students to make use of a hundreds chart to develop a sense of number relationships. Transitioning from manipulatives to pictorial representations is a key component of this chapter, and examples are provided for ways of making use of student drawings to assess conceptual understandings. In addition, using a key reading strategy such as "before," "during," and "after," teachers may find a way to provide their students with an avenue for representing mathematics that will help them build on prior knowledge and connect that knowledge to new processes.

In Chapter 4, "Using Numbers and Symbols to Represent Mathematical Ideas," the value of student-invented algorithms is explored as well as ways to use them to support student learning. Moving students from pictorial to numeric representations of the mathematics is ultimately the goal in any math classroom, but helping students make the connections and bring meaning to the math is a crucial process that cannot be rushed.

Developing student understanding of how to graph specific types of data is discussed in Chapter 5, "Using Tables and Graphs to Record, Organize, and Communicate Ideas." Whether graphing information on a picture graph or a bar graph, students need to understand and see the various data representations used so that they have the skill to choose the appropriate representations for any type of data. This chapter also shows ways to help students begin organizing solutions using tables.

Chapter 6, "Assessing Students' Representations," looks at how teachers can make decisions about assessments as they apply to the representation standard and suggestions for ways in which student representations can be assessed.

Finally, in Chapter 7, "Representation Across the Content Standards," we share lesson ideas to illustrate the representation process standard as it connects to the teaching of numbers and operations, algebra, geometry, measurement, and data and probability. Engaging students in representing their mathematical thinking in all content standards will ensure their success in applying the process in other areas.

At the end of each chapter we include reflection questions that can be used for individual reflection or to generate faculty study group discussions. The accompanying CD provides a variety of practical resources you can use to help your students more effectively represent their math ideas, including lesson ideas that can easily be adapted to meet your individual needs. Some of the activities are in the format of a worksheet and others appear as a set of teacher directions that provide lesson seeds for use in the classroom. Some activities are more teacher-directed than others, and in some cases you will need to provide additional directions to aid students as they work through the problems. This book will expand your understanding of the representation standard and will provide you with the practical resources that you'll need to implement the ideas with your students. You will also be able to personalize the activities on the CD for use in your classroom. All along the way, the "Classroom-Tested Tip" boxes provide examples of time-saving, student-motivating, and curriculum-enhancing ideas that come from the classrooms of experienced math teachers. The tips are designed to make classroom management and instruction a little easier and more meaningful and to send the message that, yes, math can be fun!

Each chapter builds on the previous chapter but can also stand alone if you are looking for one or two ideas to help math instruction in your classroom. As you read, keep this in mind: This book is written by math teachers for math teachers, with the hope that as you read at some point in time you'll have that "aha" moment and will say to yourself, "That just might work!"

Questions for Discussion

1. What does it mean to say that representation can be both a process and a product?

2. How can representing math ideas help students strengthen their understanding of math?

3. How can attention to students' representations help teachers better assess students' understanding?

4. What are some of the physical characteristics of a math classroom where students are encouraged to freely represent math ideas?

5. How can students be encouraged to communicate mathematically through representations?

6. How can the classroom environment encourage a climate of student representation?

CHAPTER 1

How Representations Support Learning

The Value of Understanding How to Represent Math Ideas

Stop for a minute, close your eyes, and picture in your mind that one math problem that frustrated you as a student. It made your palms sweat, and even today just the thought of having to tackle it can cause waves of anxiety. For most of us it probably has something to do with trains A and B leaving two stations. Today, more than ever, our students are confronted with complex problem-solving situations that can create that same level of frustration for them. Our goal as teachers is to guide them, coach them, and encourage them as they develop their understanding of numbers and improve their problem-solving skills so that they can communicate their solutions to others.

One way to achieve this goal is to show students the power of drawing pictures and using numbers, words, graphic organizers, and manipulatives alone or in combinations to bring real meaning to the mathematics. In short, the ability to create multiple representations in solving any type of math problem cannot be overestimated. When students have the confidence to represent numbers and problems in a variety of ways, they truly bring a sense of understanding and ownership to the mathematics around them. In this chapter we look at some of the tools teachers and students can use as they represent mathematical ideas and thinking.

Organizing Information

Learning to record or represent thinking in an organized way, both in solving a problem and in sharing a solution, is an acquired skill for many students (NCTM 2000). How many times have we watched a student or group of students try to work through a seemingly easy problem that they have not been able to solve? They have either missed the solution because of unorganized trials and errors or failed to see how to set up the problem correctly. Perhaps the answer was right in front of their eyes, but because of the disorganized nature of their work, it went unnoticed. This is especially true when the answer is more easily found by discovering a function or pattern in the data that ultimately leads to a solution.

Organizing solutions is not an easy process for students at the primary level. In the beginning, continuous modeling and discussion of why this process works may be the most important thing we can do to help students begin to internalize this process. Problems with multiple constraints can also give students a difficult time if they are not careful to consider the whole problem instead of trying to solve it one part at a time. Modeling the use of organizational structures is essential at this early stage, and the more opportunities students have to see how those organizers help in reaching a solution the more likely it is that they will begin to use them during their independent work. In addition, the organizers serve as record keeping tools for displaying multiple solutions to the same problem. By the time students reach second grade, they should be able to create some very basic organizational structures that enable them to see how the solutions are related.

Consider the following problem:

Driving by a farm, I saw some cows and chickens. Through the fence I counted a total of 20 legs. How many cows and chickens did I see?

This problem is well within the computational reach of students at this level, and the context should be recognizable to all students. The complexity of the problem is easily changed by increasing the number of legs or limiting the number of total animals so that only one solution is possible. This is, however, a problem that has multiple solutions, and finding one solution of 1 cow and 8 chickens should be seen as a starting point rather than the end of the problem. Students finding one answer should be challenged or guided to find additional answers. To make sure all students understand the information, time should be spent in building some background knowledge or in reviewing the number of legs of cows and chickens. Video clips, pictures, or realistic manipulatives could all be used to help students begin thinking about this problem. While the thinking and the organized record keeping needed to see a pattern in trials and errors may or may not be within the grasp of all students, it is important to provide them with a model for the organization. A word of caution: remember that providing students with a matrix or table isn't going to guarantee that they will know how to make use of this tool. Some students may stumble upon the answer without doing any type of organized thinking or record keeping. In this case, it is important to show them through discussion and modeling how the matrix or organizer would have made their work more efficient.

Students using a table such as the one in Figure 1–1 might be able to see after a couple of guesses which direction to go with their next guess. The goal is to find one of the solutions with fewer guesses and also to bring a sense of importance to putting their guesses down in an organized pattern. True, the first guess is just that—a guess. Understanding how that first guess relates to the problem as a whole and the relationship between the first and second guess to the ultimate solution is paramount. The solutions can be found more quickly (always a selling point with students) when they look at the work in a sequential manner instead of putting guesses all over the paper.

When the work is organized, the relationship of the parts of the problem is much more evident, bringing real meaning to the mathematics. Keeping track of and organizing the trials would ultimately lead them to see that each time you increase the number of cows the number of legs increases. They may not be able to express it in those terms, but that isn't important at this stage of the game. As students begin working with these types of problems, keep the answers at or close to those ever important benchmark numbers. As they experience success at this level, the range of numbers used in the problems should expand.

One of the hardest things for teachers to do is to let students work through problems independently without offering hints and more hints. Instead of providing clues to the answer, which isn't the most important part of this activity anyway, provide questions to spark their group conversations. If students are equipped with manipulatives and other tools to help them represent their thinking, they should be encouraged to keep talking to one another as they work through the problem.

There is no doubt that this type of table is useful in recording trials and errors, but it also records for the teacher the thinking that occurred as the students were engaged in solving the problem. Whether they were using manipulatives, drawing pictures, or using another problem-solving tool, the thinking is revealed in the record keeping of the trials. Going back and asking "Do you remember what you were thinking with this guess?" or "Why did you decide to try this number next?" would be impossible if students didn't keep any record of the trials and errors.

Some students may choose to solve this problem by representing the cows pictorially instead of using a matrix of trials. The challenge here is to get at students' thinking as they work through the problem. Unless a student makes a conscious effort to communicate his or her trials, there is no way to see the progression of thought. The other downfall of representing the problem pictorially is the time that it would take to arrive at the solution and the possibility that the solution would be found simply by counting each head and leg instead of looking for a pattern. Encourage students to look at the possibility of creating iconic representations to speed up the process and use what they know about doubles or skip counting as they work through the problem.

Mrs. Lemon gave her second-grade class the same problem but with 50 legs instead of 20 legs. This meant the problem had many more possible answers, a challenge at any grade, but her goal was to help students see and recognize how to use one

Animals	☒ Guess 1	☒ Guess 2	☑ Guess 3
Cows Chickens *Total Legs*	1 cow = 4 legs 5 chickens = 10 legs 4 legs + 10 legs = 14 legs Not enough legs	2 cows = 8 legs 5 chickens = 10 legs 8 legs + 10 legs = 18 legs Not enough legs	2 cows = 8 legs 6 chickens = 12 legs 8 legs + 12 legs = 20 legs Just right!

Figure 1–1 *An organized table can help students solve problems.*

solution to help find another one. When Ben approached this problem, he began by dividing his paper into six sections. Ben knew there was more than one solution, and his organizational structure allowed for a different solution in each section (Figure 1–2). Ben began by using a circle with the number 4 inside to represent one cow with 4 legs. He then drew additional circles, counting by 2s until he reached 50. He now had one solution. Since the goal of this problem was to use the information students had in one solution to help them find the next solution, Ben was guided to make two circles this time and again put the number 4 inside to represent the 4 legs of each cow. The remaining 42 legs were given to the chickens, 2 legs at a time. His work shows how he organized the trials by putting a different solution in each of the six sections of his paper. This is a great solution, and Ben obviously has the ability to build on his previous responses without starting over from scratch. This is not an easy task for students at this level, and by using circles with 4s and 2s inside, Ben showed that his

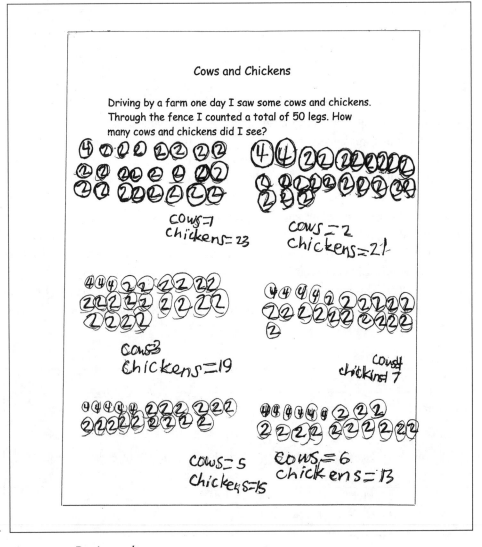

Figure 1–2 *Ben's work*

focus was on the math, not merely the artwork. The challenge here is to get students to represent the solution but also represent the steps in the solution so you can get a good picture (no pun intended!) of their thinking.

The following examples can all be used to help students see a progression of trials and errors as they work through the problems.

1. **A furniture maker was building three-legged stools and four-legged chairs. If he had 72 legs, how many stools and chairs could he make?**

2. **A bicycle maker was putting together bikes and tricycles. How many of each could he make if he had a total of 39 wheels?**

3. **Sue looked out her schoolroom window and saw kittens and ducks passing by. She counted 24 legs in all. How many kittens and ducks passed by her window?**

4. **Juan bought two boxes of spiders. In one box he counted 32 spider legs, and in the other box he counted 64 spider legs. How many spiders did he have in the two boxes? (We all know that spiders have 8 legs.)**

There are endless possibilities in working with problems of this nature. Students should find the problems easy to represent but also easy to create. Having students solve problems created by classmates adds an element of fun to the process. It also forces the creator to take care in making sure all of the numbers add up. For students experiencing difficulty in solving problems of this nature, one of the items can be removed so that only the number of one item is to be found. Stools and chairs become just chairs or just stools, and kittens and ducks become just kittens. At the same time, increasing the size of the numbers or adding a third element will meet the needs of those students needing a problem with a higher level or degree of difficulty.

Using logic problems in a math classroom gives students another opportunity to practice their step-by-step problem-solving skills. Students engaged in solving logic problems such as those dealing with deductive reasoning skills would find it almost impossible to reach an accurate conclusion in a timely fashion without the use of a table or matrix. It is essential that students have the ability to record the information given so that they can start eliminating the impossible situations first. At the same time, the use of manipulatives can help students organize their information before transferring it to the matrix.

Consider the following problem modeled in Mrs. Elwood's first-grade classroom:

At the zoo I saw four animals in a row. I saw a lion, an elephant, a bear, and a tiger. From the clues below, can you tell which one I saw first, second, third, and fourth?
    The elephant was the third animal I saw.
    The bear was next to the elephant, and I saw him before I saw the elephant.
    I didn't see the tiger first.

Logic problems such as this one provide a review of ordinal numbers and at the same time provide practice making and using a table. With the teacher's help, students

	First	Second	Third	Fourth
Bear	no	yes	no	no
Elephant	no	no	yes	no
Lion	yes	no	no	no
Tiger	no	no	no	yes

Figure 1–3 *Matrix for zoo problem*

can create a table similar to the one in Figure 1–3 to help in organizing their solution. In this example, students might choose to use a manipulative to represent each of the animals. Students can use color tiles, counters, or sorting shapes as they work through the problem, or the students themselves could be the manipulative if they choose to act out the problem. Some students may solve the problem by drawing a picture of the animals, or they may use some symbols to represent the four choices.

The key is to model the choices as they are provided and then discuss the various ways the groups represented their solutions. In this problem, Mrs. Elwood divided her students into three different groups, giving each of them a different tool to work with as they solved the problem. Group 1 used sorting animals with their matrix, Group 2 was given crayons and chart paper to draw their solution before putting it on the matrix, and Group 3 had pictures of the four animals that they taped on their shirts as they acted out the clues. In each case students worked through the problem as a small group and then everyone finished by charting their solution on the class-created matrix. The rich and lively discussion that followed gave each group a chance to talk through and demonstrate their way of solving the problem. Figure 1–3 shows the completed solution. Logic problems such as these hold so much value in training students to start with what is given and then work through the problem step by step before reaching a conclusion. The catch here is getting students to avoid premature conclusions. Some students jump to conclusions before they have sufficient information, and once they make an incorrect assumption, it is almost impossible to correctly finish the problem. Solving deductive reasoning problems such as these is a much-needed precursor skill for algebra and should be introduced in the primary grades. The value of organizing information during any mathematical situation cannot be overestimated. It is through this process that students bring meaning to the situation and communicate their understanding of the problem at hand. The hard part for students here is communicating solutions in order. Once the problem is done, do they have any idea what they did first, second, third, or last? Sometimes sticky notes or highlighter markers can be used to keep track of that information, or students can try to number their steps as they work through the problem.

In Mrs. Hayward's second-grade class, deductive reasoning puzzles are done on a regular basis, with students creating the matrices with the teacher's help. Students work in small groups as they work through the problem. Here's an example of the type of problems they solve:

Five students brought their pets to school for show and tell. The pets were a bird, a cat, a dog, a hamster, and a snake. The names of the students were Lisa, Sara, Carla, Dan, and Andy. Use the clues to determine which pet belongs to each student.

- Andy brought the snake.

- Carla's pet doesn't have fur.

- Dan doesn't have a cat or a dog.

- Lisa's pet barks at strangers.

Students working as a whole class first set the problem up by counting the number of categories needed to create the matrix. Joe commented that since there were five people and five pets, the chart needed to have a row for each. Once students had drawn the grid, they set to work labeling each of the squares. Patty wondered if it mattered whether the names went across the top or down the side. Since Mrs. Hayward wanted the students to try and answer their own questions, she offered the question to each of the small groups. They all decided that as long as one side had the names and the other side had the pets, it shouldn't matter which side they used for which category. David compared the matrix to an addition chart and said that since order didn't matter in an addition chart, it shouldn't matter here.

Using manipulatives to represent the pets, the group began putting the pets in the various squares as they read the clues. The first pet went in the box that showed Andy having a snake, and that meant that an *X* needed to go in all other boxes in that column and row because Andy can only have one pet and none of the other children could bring the snake. The problem then said Carla's pet doesn't have fur. Before putting the marker that showed Carla having the bird, the question was asked whether that meant Carla could have the snake. Charlie was quick to point out that the group had already given Andy the snake because of the first clue and that couldn't change. Carla was given the bird and *X*s were placed in all of the other animals in Carla's row. That left three animals—a cat, a dog, and a hamster—and three students. The next clue said that Dan didn't have a cat or dog; this meant that the marker for Dan needed to be placed in the box for the hamster. The group grew a little concerned when they realized they had two pets and students remaining and only one clue. They raised their hand to tell Mrs. Metzger that something had been left out, but before she could encourage them to go back and read the final clue, Alice quickly responded that they didn't need another clue since the last clue meant they could figure out one of the answers and only one other box remained empty. In reading the clue they decided neither of them had ever heard a cat bark so after a few giggles they gave Lisa the dog and Sara the cat. They finished their matrix and shared their response with the rest of the class.

Keeping the vocabulary manageable and the situations in a context that is familiar to students makes logic problems easier for students to solve. At the same time, using manipulatives as well as pictures to represent their answers goes a long way toward helping them organize their solution on the matrix.

Venn Diagrams

The Venn diagram is another tool that enables students to organize information such as the attributes of shapes, data, and numbers. It is also a valuable tool to use in problem-solving situations, and it enables students to begin classifying numbers and shapes by similarities and differences. Students just beginning to work with Venn diagrams can start with a single circle and a question or survey with only two choices: either it is or it isn't. For example, earlier grades can start with topics such as shoes that tie, shoes that don't tie; shirts with buttons, shirts with no buttons; or students who buy lunch and students who pack their lunch. With a single circle, the inside could be one of the two characteristics and the outside the other. Venn diagrams can be made more complex with the addition of more circles, allowing for additional sets or elements to be compared. In multicircle Venn diagrams, each region represents one attribute or characteristic, and the overlapping region of two or more circles represents those attributes the elements have in common. Outside the circles is yet another area that can be used to represent those numbers, shapes, or pieces of data that do not belong to any group. In addition to determining common characteristics, Venn diagrams can be used to help students with practice in representing types of numbers.

Students using the Venn diagram in Figure 1–4 would choose where to place number cards depending on whether they thought the number represented was odd or even. In addition to the numeric representations of the numbers, students should be given cards that have alternate representations such as tally marks, base ten pictures, or word names. As students communicate how they made their decisions in placing the cards, they should not only be able to say why a number fits in a region but also why it does not fit in the other region. For example: the student who chose to place 40 + 7 in the area outside the even circle might say, "The number is odd because it ends in a 7 and all even numbers must end in a 0, 2, 4, 6, or 8." By getting students to verbalize the complete thought, they are communicating a full understanding of the concept, not just a guess. Two circles could be used for this activity, but since no number is both even and odd, leaving the intersecting section empty, using one circle serves the same purpose.

Geometry is another area where students can make use of the Venn diagram. Working with attribute blocks, pattern blocks, or geometric shapes, students could be instructed to place the pieces in one of the regions of the Venn diagram using criteria that they establish. Not only do they have to choose the attributes by which to sort the shapes, but they have to be able to communicate those decisions to someone looking at their organizer.

Students in Mrs. Metzger's second-grade math class were asked to place shapes in one of the regions of the diagram and then explain their decision. Figure 1–5 shows how one student, Rachel, arranged her shapes.

It is important to remember to give students the opportunity to make these decisions and allow time for the communication instead of always giving them the characteristics of each circle. Even though a student's thinking might not always be what we are expecting, there is a great deal of value in allowing students time to work through all of these steps and to process their own decisions. In this case, Rachel wrote that she put the pieces with at least one straight side in one circle and shapes that had

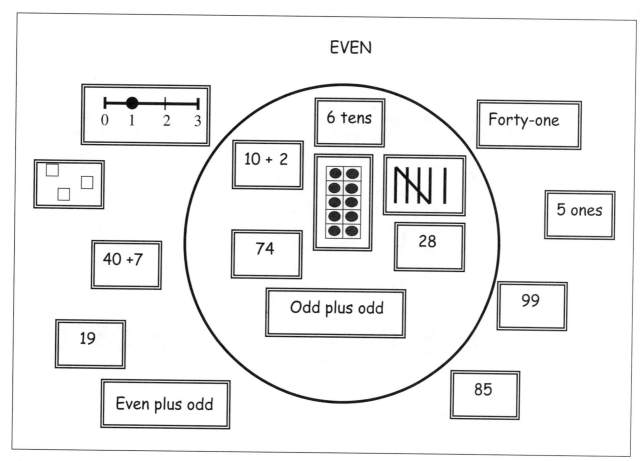

Figure 1–4 *Venn diagram showing Even and Odd*

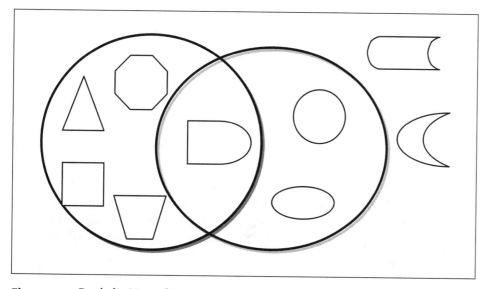

Figure 1–5 *Rachel's Venn diagram*

rounded sides in the other. She continued by saying that since one shape had both a straight side and a rounded edge, it went in the space between the two circles. She also concluded that the pieces with "dented" edges should go on the outside. It is important for students to identify the attributes of these geometric shapes that create the similarities and differences and determine whether there are other ways to group the shapes. One important question to ask is, "What characteristics did you use in placing the shapes outside the Venn?" Students might respond with comments similar to Rachel's and describe the shapes as "dented." While the concepts of concave and convex may not have been the focus of this particular lesson, students need to feel confident that when they make these decisions and communicate them appropriately, they will be accepted. The vocabulary now becomes more meaningful for the students because they have had time to internalize the concept. It is important for teachers to encourage and accept multiple answers in situations such as this so that students feel more comfortable thinking outside the box. It also provides additional opportunities for those teachable moments we all love.

CLASSROOM-TESTED TIP

If you are looking for a way to add a little fun to the use of the Venn diagram and meet the needs of some of your more kinesthetic learners, hula hoops make great Venn diagram circles. They can be placed on the floor or attached to the chalkboard. Students can represent their answers by putting the shapes, numbers, cards, manipulatives, or themselves inside the circles. If your chalkboard is also magnetic, attach small magnets to the back of the cards, and students can take turns placing answers in the appropriate sections. Purchasing a roll of magnetic tape and cutting it into pieces is an economical way to accomplish this task. This is a great way to get students up and moving!

Recording Ideas or Observations: Making the Literature and Math Connection

Students actively engaged in creating their own notes and observations bring a keen sense of understanding to the mathematics beyond that of students who simply copy teacher-created notes. To construct their own knowledge and understandings about mathematics, students need to be active participants. Passive learners aren't working to create new ideas and connections. Although it is sometimes easier to give students the information as they work through an investigation, the only person constructing meaning from the material in that case is the teacher. We can't tell students how to think; we can't be the authors of their ideas and observations. What we can do is create a community of mathematicians that sees value in being able to connect information, gleaned from investigations or experiments, to the abstract mathematical concepts that will make them successful in connecting to skills and concepts with a higher level of cognitive demand. To this end, we need to encourage students to observe, process the information, and note what is important to remember. Easier said than done! How do you create this community of self-assured mathematicians eager to observe and record with the eye of an investigative reporter?

One way is to provide an early note-taking structure to classroom lessons or investigations and encourage students to develop a system of representations that makes sense to them. Students can be supported in the beginning with templates that allow them ways to zero in on what's important. A chart, a diagram, or simply a set of guiding questions to use as they work through the process goes a long way toward helping them develop good mathematical communication.

As students are working on new material, have them set their paper up in two columns (Figure 1–6). One column would be used for the examples, and the second column could be designated as the work section; or one column could be set up for note taking, and the second column for examples and pictorial representations of the vocabulary. Several models utilize this strategy, and there are just as many names for those strategies. In one model, students divide their paper into four sections and on one section they write a word, in a second section they create an example of the vocabulary word, in the third section they draw a picture of the term, and in the fourth section students describe a real-world application for the term. Giving students the opportunity to relate the mathematics to a real-world application is important for long-term retention. Without the connection, the math is sometimes forgotten. The CD section of this book provides samples of note taking or work structures that can be used in any primary classroom.

Another way to bring structure to students' work and help them organize their work is to provide a note-taking structure that relates to the concept or, in this case, a math-related literature piece. Students working on understanding the concept of fair share would benefit from hearing the now familiar story *The Doorbell Rang*, by Pat Hutchins. As students listened to the story being read, they could use a template that resembled a cookie tray to help them record their ideas and notations. Each student in the cooperative group could have a different tray on which the individual or group would record the mathematics found in the story and connect the numbers with a picture or manipulative (see Figure 1–7). At the same time students can be

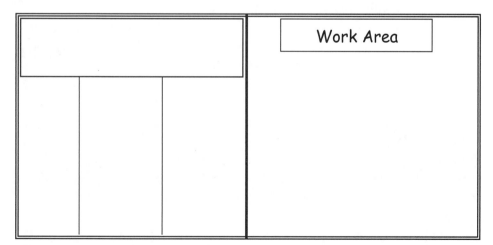

Figure 1–6 *Two-column paper setup for working on new material*

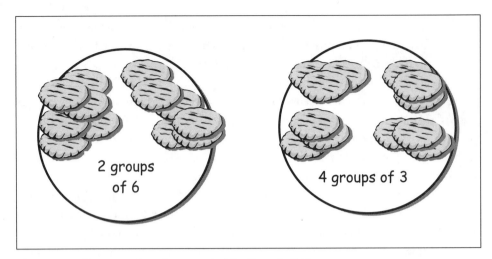

Figure 1-7 *Representing the story in* The Doorbell Rang

provided with a cookie cereal that would serve as their manipulative on the cookie tray. This record, which could help students keep track of the mathematics found in this story, would be a powerful tool in helping them make the connections between the concrete manipulative or picture and the abstract algorithm.

Here recording the mathematics could begin to take students to another level as they bring meaning and understanding to the concept of fair share. By manipulating the cookies, they can begin to see the possible combinations that make 12. As they move to this new level, they may even begin to feel confident enough to record the steps numerically or switch to an iconic representation for the manipulative instead of feeling the need to always draw realistic pictures. Using iconic representations such as circles or *X*s would certainly speed up the process.

CLASSROOM-TESTED TIP

Use plastic trays or plates made from melamine for students to record their answers. Using a dry-erase marker, students can write directly on the surface of the plate. This brings an unexpected element of fun to the activity. The writing wipes right off, and inexpensive sets of white socks work great as erasers. The sock is also a handy place to store the marker, and small plates and markers can be stored in zip-top bags for future use. Smooth placemats also work for an activity like this, although you may find you need to use dry-erase spray to eliminate the shadow marks from the surface once you erase. You'll find many uses for these plates, and seasonal plates and placemats can add an extra dimension of fun to the activity.

Perimeter and area are two related concepts that students always seem to confuse. One reason may be the way the two concepts are taught. Most curricula present the two concepts in tandem because of their relationship to one another. Do our students have enough experiences with one concept before we introduce the second concept? What if students had multiple opportunities to experience activities only with perimeter before we introduced area? Brain research tells us that students who are actively engaged in constructing meaning are more likely to retain and internalize that information. For this reason, providing students with meaningful tasks that require them to interact with the mathematics in a variety of settings will ensure students can transfer that knowledge to higher-level skills. Another great story for reinforcing the skill of recording ideas as students work through a problem is *Spaghetti and Meatballs for All!* by Marilyn Burns (1997). It is a story about a couple wanting to have a dinner for their friends and family. As the story progresses, the number of available seats (perimeter) changes, but the number of tables (area) remains constant. Activities related to this book can engage students in thinking about the way area and perimeter are related to one another and how a change in one may or may not change the other. Using this book with students also provides a real-world application of the concepts. As students listen to the story, they should be provided with manipulatives that simulate the tables and chairs. One possible manipulative for this activity are small square crackers to represent the tables and fish crackers to represent the chairs. Because the situation changes from one page to the next, it is important for students to record the situations as they change. Using large-grid graph paper, students can draw the table-and-seat arrangements from one page to the next. The discussion that takes place after the story ends is crucial to making sure students conceptualize the differences in the two concepts. Questions might include "What happens to the number of seats when the first sets of tables are pushed together?" Students can be prompted to compare the number of tables with the number of seats without making reference to the words *area* and *perimeter*. The hope here is that students will be able to make the important connection between the two concepts using a real-world example.

Communicate, Communicate, Communicate (aka Write It Down Because I Can't See Inside Your Head!)

One of the most frustrating phrases for a math teacher to hear is "I don't know how I did it. I just did it in my head." Pulling those thoughts and ideas out of our students' heads and getting them down on paper can be a challenging task to say the least, especially at the primary level when students have a limited ability to communicate using words and sentences. The trick here is to make it meaningful and somewhat fun for the students to communicate their thinking. Engaging students in opportunities to express their ideas and solutions in alternate ways can provide the motivation needed to get the ideas on paper and also play to the strengths of diverse learners.

When students are given a problem to solve or a challenge to investigate, we can encourage them to do the representation in a number of different ways. For example, one group of students could be challenged to solve the problem strictly using an appropriate algorithm; another group can show the solution pictorially using an iconic symbol or more realistic picture; another group might be challenged to find a way to chart the solution; and other groups could use manipulatives to represent the solution. Student groups can then report to the rest of the class using their representation style. Those presentations can bring about choruses of "I didn't think of that" and "That way looks way easier than our way. I'm going to try it that way next time."

Using Representations to Model a Process or Concept

It is important to remember that students must be able to construct meaning and internalize the many mathematical processes and concepts that they are expected to learn. Only through internalization of the process will it ever go beyond the rote memorization level that we all know results in "Our teacher didn't teach us that last year!" What they probably mean is that it was taught, but they just don't remember. We spend a great deal of time chastising the teachers in the previous grade levels for not making sure students know their addition facts, how to count, or how to recognize patterns instead of reflecting on our own practice. Are we guilty of doing the same things? Students provided with opportunities to internalize a process through modeling and problem-solving situations instead of just practicing the process over and over again are much more likely to remember and to be able to apply the process when confronted with higher-level problems. "Students need to work with each representation extensively in many contexts as well as move between representations in order to understand how they can use a representation to model mathematical ideas and relationships" (NCTM 2000).

Grades preK–2 are critical years for students as they refine and extend their skills with addition, subtraction, place value, and geometry. One of the most widely used manipulative models for place value is base ten blocks. One of the reasons these work so well is that they are already proportional in size and come with ready-made grouped sets of tens, hundreds, and thousands. Students using these models to learn addition, subtraction, and place value can literally see the relationships between the values by comparing the sizes of the pieces. Trading in ten ones for one ten or ten tens for one hundred becomes more meaningful because of the size relationship of the pieces. The physical size of the pieces can serve as a cue to the number relationship between the values. However, that same model becomes more difficult to use once the numbers students are working with become larger and more complex. There are times when students can be encouraged to make the problem smaller, but that is sometimes not appropriate for the work at hand. It is important to find ways to help students generalize the magnitude of numbers and place values beyond what they can see with the standard manipulative models. For this reason, we need to engage them in activities that showcase the size of large numbers, and at the same time we need to make sure they can relate to the size of those numbers that are less than one.

Developing number sense during the primary grades using the models at hand can help students as they work with larger numbers, but generalizations are not enough. How many classes have started collecting a million bottle caps only to find that the task was too unwieldy or just impossible from a standpoint of finding some place to store the collected caps? Perhaps an easier activity would be to collect ten and then one thousand and then work to help students generalize the number using the grouping model. As students collect the bottle caps, they need to find a system for keeping track of the amounts. Using tally marks allows students to group quantities of the items as they are collected and then translate the symbolic representation to numerical representation. A number of literature books, such as Jerry Pallotta's *Count to a Million* (2003), David Schwartz's *How Much Is a Million?* (1997), and Helen Nolan's *How Much, How Many, How Far, How Heavy, How Long, How Tall Is 1,000?* (2001), focus on larger quantities and help students gain a true sense of the size of those numbers. Using these books in a math classroom helps make the math-literature connection. Additional titles are listed in the Resources for Teachers section of this book.

The Role of the Teacher

One of the most important things to remember about graphic organizers or any other organizational tool students might use is that students need to see how the tool can be used for multiple purposes. For example, if students see a Venn diagram used only in reading class for comparing and contrasting, they won't be likely to use it in math class. Seeing the similarities and differences in math concepts and processes is a crucial process in helping students remember and internalize them. Students duplicating an organizer in the same manner that they have seen it modeled may be getting meaning from that process (Figure 1–8). On the other hand, they may just be copying what they have seen the teacher produce. Allow students an opportunity not only

Figure 1–8 *By organizing her work, Jessica is better able to keep track of all of her solutions.*

to see various organizers in use but also to choose which ones they want to use for a given situation.

Questions for Discussion

1. Venn diagrams and matrices help students organize their thoughts and trials as they work through problem-solving situations. What other graphic organizers lend themselves to this best practice?

2. What other benefits can be found in making the math-literature connection?

3. What problems encourage students to respond using multiple representations?

4. How can graphic organizers be used to differentiate a problem-solving situation?

CHAPTER 2

Using Manipulatives to Model and Illustrate Key Math Concepts

Mathematical representations help provide students with a perspective on phenomena.

—Sara P. Fisher and Christopher Hartmann, "Math through the Mind's Eye"

Modeling Ideas with Manipulatives

The National Council of Teachers of Mathematics recommends that teachers should employ "representations to model and interpret physical, social, and mathematical phenomena" (NCTM 2000, 70) and that students should use mathematical representations to organize their thinking and reflect on numerical or geometric information. In the previous chapter, we discussed how different representations support mathematical learning. As students become more comfortable creating models of their thinking, they build a repertoire of strategies from which to pull when faced with a novel task. "The very act of generating a concrete representation establishes an image of the knowledge in students' minds," write Marzano, Pickering, and Pollack (2001, 78). In this chapter, we look at the power of using manipulatives to help students develop their own understanding of mathematical concepts, as well as the role of the teacher in developing meaningful, appropriate tasks with manipulatives.

Teachers today have many different types of manipulatives from which to choose when planning math instruction: colorful centimeter cubes, Unifix cubes, one-inch tiles, base ten blocks, fraction circles, geometric solids, two-color counters, pattern blocks, and the list goes on. The use of them as math tools can give us great insight into a child's thinking about mathematical concepts, as well as their conceptual understandings and misunderstandings. It is only by seeing how a child approaches a problem and by listening to what he or she says about it that we gain important information that can guide our instruction.

With this in mind, consider the following scenario (see Figure 2–1):

> It is early in the year in your second-grade class, and you are interested in seeing how flexible your students are in thinking about numbers. You choose to use base ten blocks, with which your students are familiar, because they offer a concrete way of representing the value of a number. You ask them to show you the number 36. Most students use three rods and six units to represent the number. You then ask them to show the number another way. Some students look at you with confusion, while others build the number using two rods and sixteen units and still others use one rod and twenty-six units or simply thirty-six units.

This quick, informal assessment gives a piece of information that can be used to guide further instruction. Students who can see the number 36 in only one way (e.g., three tens and six ones) need more experiences with finding different ways to represent a certain quantity. Continuing with the quick assessment, you then ask them to show what ten less than thirty-six looks like. Again, there are a variety of responses: some students take a rod away, indicating that they understand conservation of number (i.e., that a rod in this case represents ten and they do not need to recount the units that make up the rod), while others try to count out ten units. Some are able to do this if they showed the quantity thirty-six with sixteen or more units, but if they were able

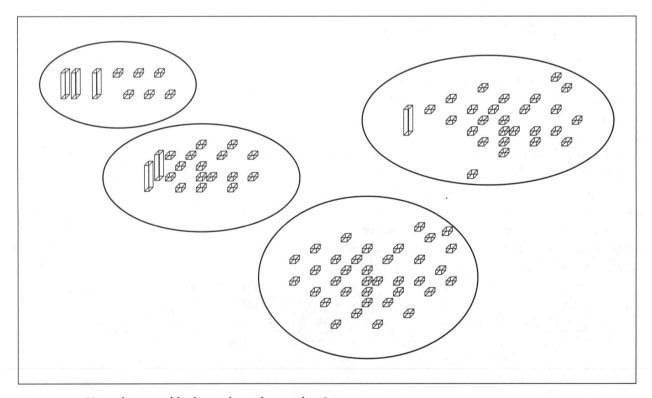

Figure 2–1 *Using base ten blocks to show the number 36*

to name thirty-six only with three rods and six units, they cannot figure out what to do next. The ability to think flexibly about numbers and to represent them in different ways is a skill that we should work to develop in our primary students. It will better enable students to deconstruct and reconstruct numbers later on, which will assist them with operating on a number (adding, subtracting, multiplying, dividing), as well as with algebraic thinking.

CLASSROOM-TESTED TIP

When using base ten blocks (see Figure 2–2) to introduce larger and smaller numbers, play a listening game with the kids. Designate which block is worth one (e.g., the small unit cube if working with whole numbers or the large cube if working with fractions or decimals). Drop the blocks, one at a time, on an overhead or table, and ask the children to guess the value of the block you dropped. For example, if the small unit cube represents one, then when the kids hear the flat dropped, they will shout out, "One hundred!" This reinforces the size of the different numbers in an aural way in addition to a visual one.

Building Understanding Through the Use of Manipulatives

When students can see and manipulate ideas, they gain a better understanding of those ideas. Consider the relationship between addition and subtraction in this problem:

Lowell bought two bunches of flowers for his mom. One bunch had 19 flowers in it. Together, both bunches had 43 flowers. How many flowers were in the second bunch?

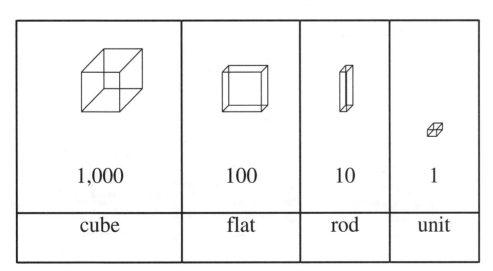

1,000	100	10	1
cube	flat	rod	unit

Figure 2-2 *Base ten blocks*

To complete this task, students were given the opportunity to use small flower-shaped erasers or cubes to represent the flowers. One student, Alison, created a "bunch" of nineteen flowers using the manipulatives, and then added one flower at a time until the total number of flowers equaled forty-three. She counted up how many flowers she had added to find out the unknown: twenty-four flowers in the second bunch. She then created a written representation of the work she had done with manipulatives (see Figure 2–3). Alison used an addition model to solve this problem. In looking at her work, we can see that she is capable of creating a pictorial representation of her understanding of the problem and that this helped her solve the problem. A learning goal for Alison might be to find a more efficient way of "drawing" the problem: for example, using circles or lines to represent each flower rather than drawing

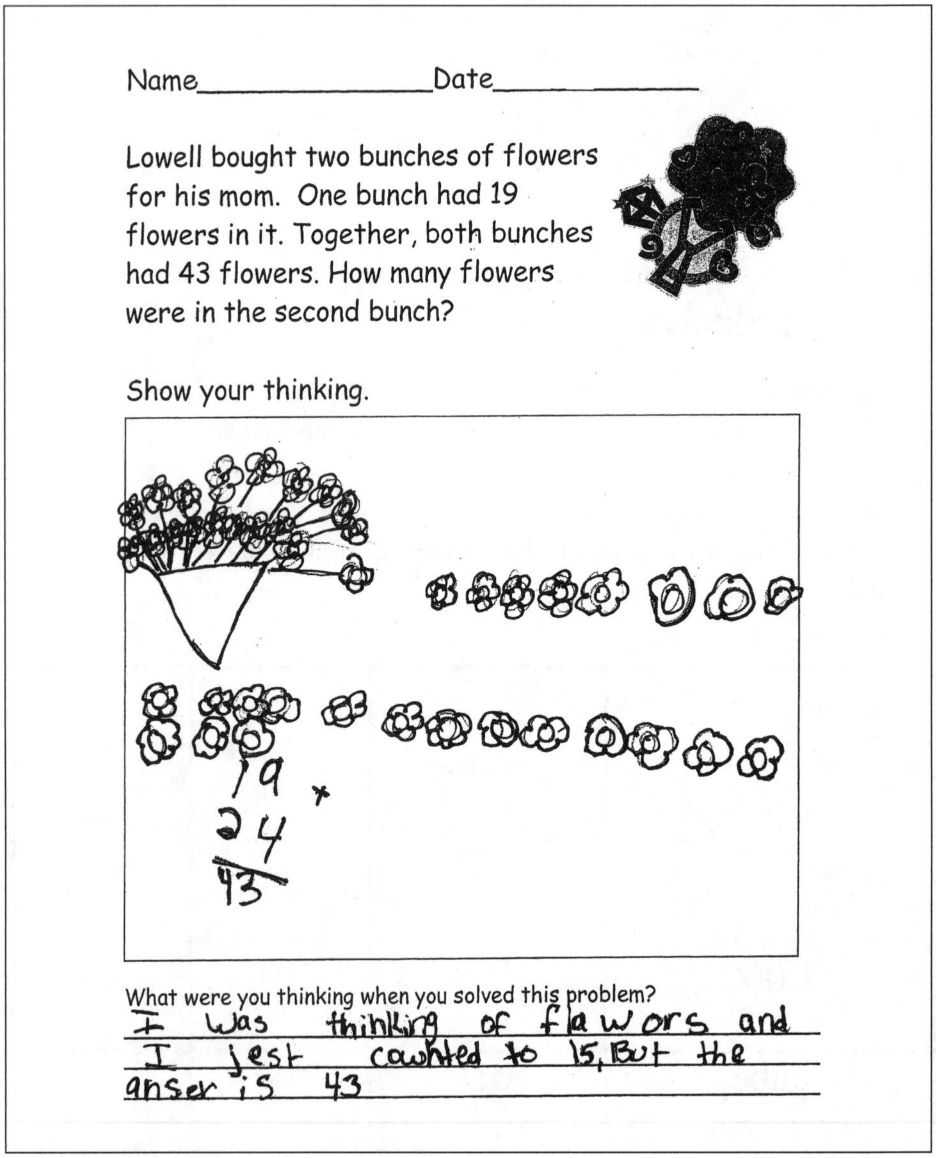

Name_____Date_____

Lowell bought two bunches of flowers for his mom. One bunch had 19 flowers in it. Together, both bunches had 43 flowers. How many flowers were in the second bunch?

Show your thinking.

What were you thinking when you solved this problem?
I was thinking of flawors and I jest cownted to 15, but the anser is 43

Figure 2–3 *Alison's work to solve the problem*

out forty-three flowers. Also, while she clearly solved the problem and even wrote an equation to represent what she had done, she did not clearly label the answer, which would be another goal for her. Kyle, on the other hand, approached the problem in a different way. He made a group of forty-three flowers, and then he counted out nineteen, leaving the unknown quantity: twenty-four. Kyle used a subtraction model to solve the same problem. Still other students did not understand the problem: Russell counted out nineteen flowers, and then he counted out another group of forty-three flowers. He put them together and concluded that the answer was sixty-two flowers. When asked if his answer made sense, he recounted each group and put them together to arrive at the same total, sixty-two, and his response was yes, his answer made sense. He was using an addition model to solve the problem, but he did not have a clear understanding of what the problem was asking.

By selecting a few students who correctly solved the problem in different ways to share and discuss their strategies with the class, students will see that they can solve this problem using addition or subtraction, and they will begin to see the relationship between the two. Manipulatives help with this discovery by allowing students to experiment with different problem-solving strategies while not being overly concerned with what the "correct" approach might be (read more about this in Chapter 4).

Another area of mathematics that is best learned with physical models is fractions. When our students are learning beginning fraction concepts, we should use many different kinds of manipulatives to make it more concrete and interesting for them. The mathematical idea of "halving" something is generally introduced in kindergarten or first grade. A natural way to represent halves is with food: we can cut an apple in half and clearly see that the two parts are equal, and when put back together, create a whole. Or we can take a chocolate bar, break it into two equal parts, and call each part half. These representations make sense to children and help them to develop their own understanding of the concept of one-half. Another fun, hands-on way to play with the idea of one-half is to use counters such as plastic teddy bears, frogs, and so on. Given a small group of these counters, children can experiment with dividing the total into two equal groups, with each group representing half of the whole. We can also ask students to use a set of two-color counters or a number line model to demonstrate one-half, as seen in Figure 2–4. Using a model helps reinforce the concept that fractions show *relationships* between a whole and its parts.

In each of the representations in Figure 2–4, children can see that half (one of two equal parts or groups) of each whole is shaded, and that while each representation differs from the others in form and area, they all show the same relationship of parts to the whole, and therefore each is called one-half.

We want our students eventually to be familiar and comfortable using three models of fractions: area/region, length/measurement, and set. Consider the following task:

Draw a picture to represent each of the following situations.

▪ **Aaron's plant is 2 inches tall. Christine's plant is twice as tall. How tall is Christine's plant?** [length/measurement model]

▪ **Braddock Elementary's first-grade classes are planting a flower garden. In one-fourth of the garden they will grow red roses. In another fourth, they will grow**

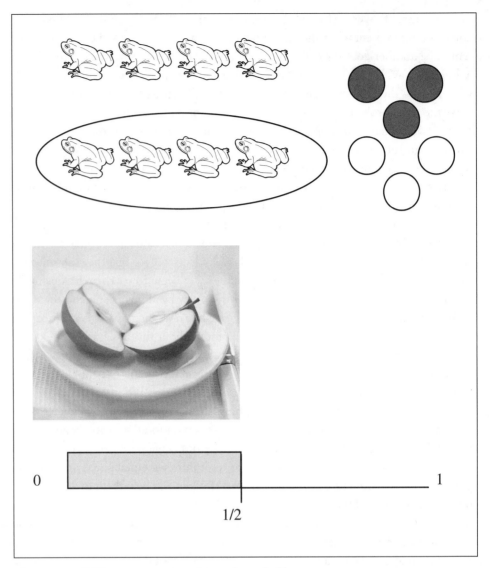

Figure 2–4 *Different representations of one-half*

yellow daisies. In the third fourth, they will grow purple pansies, and in the last fourth they will grow pink carnations. Show what their garden looks like. [area/region model]

> Tammy has six cookies to share with a friend. If Tammy and her friend each get half of the cookies, how many will each one get? [set model]

Each of these situations can best be represented by a particular fraction model. Over time, we want our students to become experienced enough with the different models that they can correctly choose the best representation for a fraction situation.

CLASSROOM-TESTED TIP

Work fractions and percents into your everyday language, even if students have only a minimal understanding of the concepts. After giving whole-group instructions, look for table groups to be ready and describe their representation in different ways:

▪ I see one-fourth of the students at John's table are ready.

▪ Half of the students at Grace's table are ready.

▪ 100 percent of Gabriela's table is ready!

Moving from the Concrete to the Abstract

In geometry, manipulatives are particularly useful as students begin to explore polygons and solids and to classify them according to attributes, as seen in this task:

Sort your polygon tiles according to different attributes and give each group labels. Record your groups on paper by tracing the polygon tiles.

By allowing students to conduct this investigation with manipulatives (in this case, polygon tiles), we give students the ability to see and feel the different attributes of each tile, and they have the flexibility to move tiles in and out of groups until they are satisfied with their groupings. Some questions we might ask students as they complete this task include "Why did you sort them the way you did?" "Could you have sorted them in a different way?" and "Could some shapes have fit in more than one group?" In addition, by asking students to record their work, we are helping them move from the concrete to the abstract. This is an important step in students' growth as young mathematicians. By being able to work with manipulatives and then create paper-and-pencil representations of their work, students begin to create pictures in their mind from which they will draw as they are presented with more and more difficult tasks. In Figure 2–5 a group of students is considering why some tiles fit in the circle but others do not. As they worked, they discussed the task, making comments like these:

▪ These all have four sides, but none of these do.

▪ This one has four sides, but it doesn't look like these ones because it's kind of squished.

▪ These all look like squares.

Figure 2–5 *Students work together to determine which shapes belong in the circle.*

This activity provided students with a hands-on way to explore attributes of geometrical figures, and by having the polygon tiles to work with, the students had a physical model with which to explain their thinking to their peers and to help them justify their thinking.

Geoboards are another excellent model for investigating geometry concepts. They are engaging and novel to students, increasing their motivation and therefore heightening their learning. In second grade, as students begin to explore the concept of transformations, geoboards offer a hands-on way to create figures, predict what the figures will look like if reflected, translated, or rotated, and then check to see if their predictions are correct. Here is an activity in which students experiment with rotational symmetry:

> On your geoboard, create a nonsquare rectangle. Predict what the rectangle will look like if rotated a one-quarter turn, a one-half turn, and a three-quarters turn. Record your predictions on geoboard paper, and then test your predictions by turning your geoboard to see how they compare.

In this activity, students are engaging in spatial learning as they visualize what the rectangle will look like if rotated. They actually rotate the entire geoboard, rather than the rectangle, to see what changes will occur without touching the shape itself.

Again, students are asked to complete a task using concrete materials, and then they must move toward a more abstract representation of the concept. As Marzano et al. (2001) pointed out, the very act of creating a model of the knowledge enhances student understanding of a concept.

Manipulatives and Student Learning Styles

Research shows that humans better retain that which they do rather than that which they hear or see. In other words, when students are actively, hands-on engaged with their learning, we can feel confident that they are creating more long-term knowledge and understandings than if they experienced concepts passively. Generally speaking, there are six identified learning styles:

■ *Auditory:* Students with this strength are able to recall what they hear and usually prefer oral instructions. They enjoy talking and interviewing, giving oral reports, and listening to recorded books.

■ *Visual:* Students with this learning style are able to recall what they see and prefer written instructions. They learn by observing and enjoy computer graphics, graphs, charts, diagrams, graphic organizers, and text with many pictures.

■ *Tactile:* Students who are tactile learners learn best by touching. They learn best through the use of manipulatives. They enjoy drawing, making models, and following instructions to make something.

■ *Kinesthetic:* Students with this strength learn by touching or manipulating objects. They need to involve their bodies in learning. They enjoy playing games that involve their whole body, movement activities, making models, and following instructions to make something.

■ *Global:* These learners do not like to be bored. They learn best when information is presented in an interesting manner using attractive materials. Cooperative learning strategies work well with these students. They enjoy computer programs, games, and group activities.

■ *Analytical:* Students with this learning style like to plan and organize their work. They focus on details and are logical. They learn best when goals are clear, requirements are spelled out, and information is presented in sequential steps.

Using manipulatives and other forms of representation appeal to at least five of these learning styles: visual, tactile, kinesthetic, global, and analytical. Visual learners benefit from seeing and creating models, diagrams, pictures, and other forms of representation as they experience mathematical concepts. Tactile and kinesthetic learners appreciate being able to touch manipulatives and use them to make models of the mathematical concepts they are learning. Students with a global learning style enjoy using virtual manipulatives on the computer, participating in group activities that require the use of concrete manipulatives, and being actively engaged as they create their own understandings of math concepts. Finally, analytical learners enjoy planning and organizing their work and apply logic to their use of materials as they work to solve mathematical problems.

As we become more cognizant of the different ways in which students learn, we can feel confident that by using manipulatives and other representations we are reaching a majority of our students and tapping into their strengths. Students will be more likely to create lasting understandings of concepts if they learn them in hands-on, active ways.

CLASSROOM-TESTED TIP

Good Questioning

Asking questions is an essential part of our approach to teaching and assessing. By asking probing questions, we require students to articulate their thoughts and strategies for solving a problem. Try to include open-ended questions such as these:

- How did you solve it?

- Why did you solve it that way?

- Why do you think you're correct?

- How could you have solved it a different way?

Manipulatives Can Influence Understanding

In their book *Making Sense*, James Hiebert et al. (1997) argue that the tools that students use can result in students constructing different understandings about concepts. Take, for example, multidigit addition and subtraction. Students who have had many experiences with base ten blocks likely see numbers as made up of units of tens and units of ones, and they will be more likely to construct an understanding that involves adding those units together and then making adjustments. For example, a student who sees the different units in a number may add 26 plus 37 in this way:

$$26 + 37 \rightarrow 20 + 30 = 50 \rightarrow 6 + 7 = 13 \rightarrow 50 + 13 = 63$$

On the other hand, children who engage in many counting activities and use hundreds boards will more likely see the counting sequence in an addition or subtraction problem:

$$26 + 37 \rightarrow 20 + 10 = 30 \rightarrow 30 + 10 = 40 \rightarrow 40 + 10 = 50 \rightarrow 50 + 6 = 56 \rightarrow 56 + 7 = 63$$

Each student, based on his own constructed understandings, would then develop his own alternative algorithm for the process. Some students may even have difficulty understanding the traditional algorithm because it does not reflect their understandings about numbers. In some cases, it is difficult for students to move from one concept of numbers to another. That is to say, if their early experiences have been with base ten materials, they are likely to have a units view of multidigit numbers, and they may have difficulty using a counting strategy, even with supports such as number lines. The reverse is true of students whose early experiences were with a counting approach to numbers.

The importance of this phenomenon is that teachers must recognize that the tools they select for their students to use will likely affect the understandings they construct. There is no one correct understanding about a concept, so teachers need not be overly concerned with selecting the *right* tool to help develop students' understanding. Rather, they need to be cognizant of the way in which the tools they choose can influence understandings about a concept, and it would be beneficial to have a conversation with colleagues about this topic when deciding which tools to select.

CLASSROOM-TESTED TIP

Collecting Math Tools

At the beginning of the year, send a letter home to parents (see the Representation Toolkit section on the CD) explaining how you use math tools to help their children develop mathematical understandings. Ask them to begin collecting different items that can be incorporated into their children's learning, and describe possible uses, such as the following:

- *Craft sticks* can be used to explore the concepts of vertical, horizontal, parallel, perpendicular, right angle, acute angle, obtuse angle, and so on.

- *Beans* can be used to explore volume and capacity or as counters and markers.

- *Egg cartons* can be used to explore addition, subtraction, multiplication, division, and fractions, and they can be cut down to serve as a ten frame.

- *Colorful plastic eggs* can be used to explore addition, subtraction, multiplication, division, and fractions.

- *Small plastic figures*, such as dinosaurs or toy cars, can be used to sort, to explore fractions of a set, or as prompts for creating story problems.

- *Coins* can be used to explore money concepts; plus they're less expensive than buying plastic coins.

- *Small, interesting boxes and containers*, such as cosmetics packaging, can be used to explore the properties of solid figures or the concept of volume, and the numbers on them can be used to create math problems.

■ *Everyday containers*, such as milk jugs, soda bottles, and water bottles, can be used to explore volume and capacity and serve as visual benchmarks.

■ *Single-serve frozen dinner trays* can be used to hold manipulatives such as number cubes and tiles during a lesson.

■ *Plastic sealable bags* of various sizes can be used to create small sets of manipulatives.

■ *Ribbon and yarn* can be used to explore measurement concepts or to create a number line.

■ *Wrapping paper* can be used during measurement problem-solving activities.

Many of these items can be found around the house, and most parents would be happy to have the opportunity to contribute to their child's instructional program. Invite parents into the classroom to learn ways in which they can use items at home to support their children's mathematical learning.

Manipulatives and Technology

Walk into any classroom and you may see many different ways in which students are using representation to help develop their mathematical understanding: manipulatives such as base ten materials or geometric solids; graphic organizers such as Venn diagrams or tables; and more and more, we see students using technology to represent their thinking. Tools such as virtual manipulatives and interactive white boards are opening up endless possibilities for teachers and students to create meaning about mathematical topics.

Patricia Moyer, Johnna Bolyard, and Mark Spikell, in their article titled, "What Are Virtual Manipulatives?" (2002), established a definition of virtual manipulatives. They distinguish between "static" and "dynamic" visual representations of concrete manipulatives. Static visual representations are merely pictures on the screen. They resemble concrete manipulatives, but they cannot be acted upon in the same way as concrete manipulatives. For example, students may see a picture of two sets of base ten blocks and be asked to add them. With concrete manipulatives, they would be able to combine the two sets, exchanging some blocks for others as necessary, resulting in a sum that was represented by one group of the combined blocks. However, with static visual representations, there is no potential for students to do any manipulating; they are simply looking at a picture, much as they would see in a textbook or on the overhead projector, and must do the work mentally (or by creating their own representation with blocks or with paper and pencil).

Dynamic visual representations offer teachers and students many of the same opportunities for manipulating as concrete materials do. Students can manipulate tiles or pattern blocks, for example, to illustrate the geometric concept of symmetry. When learning about subtraction with multidigit numbers, students might use a tool, such as a mallet on the virtual manipulative website (www.arcytech.org/java/b10blocks), to "break apart" the larger blocks into their smaller components and move them around. The largest online collection of virtual manipulatives can be found at Utah State University's National Library of Virtual Manipulatives (http://nlvm.usu.edu/en/nav/index.html). This website offers teachers and students learning opportunities in the five NCTM strands: numbers and operations, algebra, geometry, measurement, and data analysis and probability. It includes lesson plans for teachers and ready-made activities for students. One advantage dynamic manipulatives have over concrete materials is that the shortage problem we sometimes face when we're teaching a lesson is eliminated. Online there is no shortage of blocks or other math tools; students can create a representation using as many pattern blocks as they want without worrying about running out of hexagons, for example, as sometimes happens when we have a class set of manipulatives that we have split into smaller sets for group work.

An interactive white board also offers a different perspective for students when manipulating visual representations. Any virtual manipulative website can be displayed on the large white board, and the dynamic visual representations can be engaged and controlled by the user in a way that is easily visible to peers. For example, when learning about different shapes and their attributes, a second-grade student can click on and drag shapes to group them in different ways. Figure 2–6 shows the work a first-grade student did on an interactive white board to illustrate an addition problem, and it provided her with the opportunity to move and be active during the lesson. Interactive white boards have many uses and provide us with another way to engage our students and to represent concepts in an interesting and active way.

Figure 2–6 *A student uses an interactive white board to illustrate an addition problem.*

The Role of the Teacher

The teacher's importance when using manipulatives to build understanding cannot be overstated. We are responsible for modeling how to use the manipulatives, asking questions to push understanding, selecting meaningful tasks, and moving students from the concrete to the abstract. It's very important that teachers have a deep understanding of the mathematics they are teaching. How many times have we gone through the motions of teaching a concept without really getting it ourselves? In addition, we need to be able to understand students' thinking, identify misconceptions, and clear up confusions. This can be done only if we thoroughly understand the mathematics we are teaching. Community colleges, online courses, and district-sponsored training, just to name a few, provide opportunities for us to enhance our knowledge of mathematics content and improve our efficacy in teaching math.

As part of our beginning-of-the-year procedures and throughout the year, we model the behaviors we expect of our students so that they are safe and successful. Using math manipulatives is no exception. If we want our students to use them as tools and not toys, we must allow them first to discover the possibilities of how they might be used in a supervised way. For example, pattern blocks are a popular manipulative for learning about geometry, fractions, and other concepts. These colorful blocks are so appealing to learners, both younger and older, and offer so many possibilities in terms of designing and patterning, that we would be mistaken to pass them out to students and jump right into a lesson without giving them exploration time first. Students need time to play, if you will, with the items that they will be using later as tools. It's likely many of us know firsthand what happens when we don't conduct a guided discovery of a math tool: the students are so engaged in playing with the manipulatives, or in the mere temptation of playing with them, that we have to continually stop to redirect them just to get through the lesson! By allowing them a few minutes to satisfy their natural curiosity, we are setting our students up for a more meaningful learning experience. Another way to facilitate this exploration is to leave baskets of the manipulatives out and allow students to handle them when they have free time.

Base ten blocks, another popular math manipulative, reinforce the concept that our number system uses a system of ten. However, we cannot assume that children will immediately recognize and understand the relationship between the blocks. For example, to see that a rod is worth ten because it is made of ten unit cubes, many children will need to actually lay ten units next to a rod to see the equivalency. The same applies to the relationship between the units, rods, and flats. In addition, we must assist children in learning conservation of number; children must learn that a rod is always worth ten (when the unit is worth one), and therefore it is not necessary to count each part of the rod to determine its value every time. These are just some of the critical roles we play when helping students become proficient in using manipulatives to explore a mathematical concept.

Questions for Discussion

1. How can "seeing" ideas through the use of manipulatives help our students in their growing mathematical understandings?

2. What are some ways in which we can help our students move from the concrete to the abstract? Why is this important?

3. How does the use of manipulatives and other representations appeal to the different learning styles of our students?

4. How can the tools we select to use with our students influence their understandings about a concept?

5. What is the role of the teacher in using manipulatives to teach mathematics?

Using Pictures and Diagrams to Represent Mathematical Thinking

Students who represent the problem in some way are more likely to see important relationships than those who consider the problem without a representation.

— National Council of Teachers of Mathematics,
Principles and Standards for School Mathematics

Pictures and Diagrams

Student use of manipulatives is essential in developing the conceptual understanding of the mathematics at hand, so it isn't an instructional strategy that should be treated lightly. However, as students move toward more abstract thinking, we need to increase their confidence and abilities in using alternative methods of bringing meaning to their math. As the mathematics becomes more complex, students may find manipulatives less helpful and that they need to rely more on alternative representations that make the problem-solving process more efficient. For this reason, it is important that the representation stage be introduced and modeled while the manipulatives are still on the desk. This allows students an opportunity to make the connection between the two. For primary students, communicating their thinking and understanding of mathematics can be accomplished more quickly when they use some type of pictorial representation. In fact, students should be shown and encouraged to use a variety of those same representations. We must remember that the pictorial representations will have meaning for students only if they have a deep understanding and mastery of the purpose and use of the concrete representations. Research by Piaget confirms the necessity of moving students through these stages, not skipping over them. We need to help students build the bridge between the two. In this chapter we focus on some specific uses for pictures and diagrams as ways to represent mathematics and look at how students can use those representations to communicate their solutions.

Some of the early concepts for primary students include ordinal numbers and positional words. Using pictures and diagrams, students can model their thinking and represent their solutions beyond just circling a picture. Story mats are pictures that have a variety of elements focusing on a theme or event. For example, at the beginning of the school year, a story mat might be used that shows students in an apple orchard or a pumpkin patch. During the winter season the story mat might show a snow scene with snowmen and children on sleds, and spring and summer scenes could show children at the beach or enjoying other outdoor activities. The most important aspect of the picture is that the elements need to be carefully placed so that questions and directions can be used that get at the math concepts. In Mrs. Brinsfield's kindergarten classroom, students are given a story mat that shows children at the beach with buckets of various sizes and colors. Each student is given a supply of foam cutouts that include starfish, fish, and pieces of coral. As Mrs. Brinsfield gives directions, students represent their answers by placing their cutouts on the story mat. She might tell them to place two starfish in the third bucket or place a piece of coral under the buckets. Her directions might include putting a starfish in the first bucket, two starfish in the second bucket, and three starfish in the third bucket. As students progress, the directions can grow in complexity to include concepts such as even and odd. Students might be asked to place an odd number of fish in the water and an even number of starfish on the sand. Mrs. Brinsfield uses a demonstration mat to model placement of the cutouts, and she asks the students to describe what she has done. If she has three starfish in one of the buckets, students might respond with there are an odd number of starfish in the second bucket. Story mats can be created from a variety of pieces of clipart or found in any primary book or coloring book. By using the foam cutouts, the pictures can be used from year to year, and they do add an element of fun to the activity.

The hundreds chart is a staple in all primary classrooms. As a tool for modeling numbers and helping students visualize the relationship those numbers have to one another, it is invaluable, and a number of activities are designed to support this tool. One such activity has students looking at ways to find the mystery number. Before transitioning to the hundreds chart, students in Diana Churchman's second-grade class use the base ten blocks to model numbers and find a mystery number by adding or subtracting values of tens and ones. Once students have had many opportunities to see the relationships between these numbers, Mrs. Churchman provides students with their own hundreds chart and a place marker to move around the board as she gives them clues to the mystery numbers. Modeling the process on the class-sized hundreds chart, students can check their accuracy. As she announces the starting number, 39, Mrs. Churchman looks around to first see if everyone has his or her marker on the correct starting point, and then she proceeds with the clues to find the mystery number. She tells the students to move their marker to a number that is 4 tens more than the number 39. It is important to observe how students determined not only where their marker should land but also how they determined the mystery number. Are students merely counting out forty spaces, or are they using the marker and counting down the hundreds chart 4 tens? Once all students have their new answer, she has them write that answer on their dry-erase boards and then has them communicate their process. It's the process that takes center stage at this point. Students who have a keen sense of the relationship of place value will be able to move their counter down four spaces instead of counting out forty spaces. In this case there seems to be a little bit of both happening in her room, so she has a student come to the front and not only model his thinking but explain why he knew counting four groups of tens could be done in four moves instead of forty. Later on in the year, Mrs. Churchman begins to pull segments out from the hundreds chart so that instead of seeing the whole chart, they can only see a part of that hundreds chart. She places a few numbers on the chart and then a question mark to signal where the mystery number is located. Students use a blank grid and work together to see if they can find the mystery number. Rather than tell her the answer only, she has students give her the clues that determine the spot where the number is located. Sophia gave this clue: starting at 22, move your counter to a number that is ten more plus two. Jordon, on the other side of the room, offered his solution: starting at forty-two, move your marker to the space that is ten less and two more. Both solutions worked, and when Luke said he did the same as Jordon but not in the same order, Mrs. Churchman used this example to ask the class if it made a difference if they were to add the two first and then take ten less (Figure 3–1).

During the discussion, students are asked to pull out their base ten blocks and check to see what they discover. It would have been much easier for Mrs. Churchman to give them the answer, but knowledge just given isn't as easily remembered as knowledge discovered. This is about discovery, and what the students find is that in this case it doesn't matter. Her question to them now is, "Will this always be the case?" Rather than answer that question now, she challenges them to consider that process as she tries other clues. Some of Mrs. Churchman's clues include the following:

1. Starting on 23, move your marker to a number that is 3 tens plus 1 more than 23.

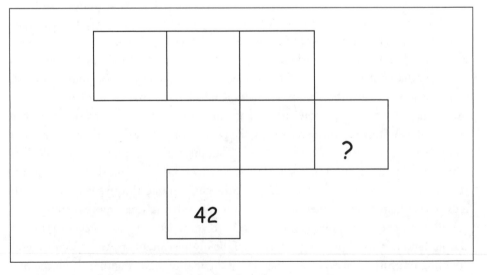

Figure 3-1 *Find the mystery number in this chart.*

2. Starting on 76, move your marker to the number that is 1 ten and 5 ones less than 76.

3. Starting on the only 3 digit number on the board, move your marker to the number that is 4 tens less than that starting number.

The hundreds chart can provide students with multiple opportunities to relate numbers to one another, and as they advance in their skills, additional concepts such as multiples can be modeled using the hundreds chart.

Moving from Manipulatives to Pictures: Why Transition?

Students in grades preK–2 move through several mathematical stages in these four years. They begin building and refining their skills with counting and one-to-one correspondence, place value, adding and subtracting basic facts, and applying those skills to three- and four-digit addition and subtraction before moving toward the understanding of multiplication as repeated addition. Although certain manipulatives may be useful with whole-number operations of manageable size, they become increasingly cumbersome and sometimes downright difficult, if not impossible, to manage with larger and more complex numbers. When working with complex numbers, students have a choice of trying to make the problem easier by using smaller, more manageable numbers so they can still use the manipulatives or using some type of pictorial or graphic representation that can be applied to the situation and thereby allow them to represent and solve the problem as it is written. Either method will work. Teachers need to model both processes so that students become proficient in working with complex numbers in problem-solving situations.

The types of representations that students choose to use can vary widely. For this reason it is important to allow them the freedom to invent a representation that is meaningful for them. Some students may need to draw realistic pictures to help in solving the problem, but as numbers become more complex, student representations may by necessity become more iconic. Many times, students initially choose to painstakingly draw representations to help them visualize the problem that are so realistic that they spend all of their time drawing pictures and lose sight of the mathematics involved. This is especially true at the primary level. It's like moving students from Rembrandts to Picassos. Progressing toward more symbolic representations provides students with multiple opportunities to expand their tool kit of strategies when their thinking allows them to make the connections between those symbols and actual shapes.

What Does a Picture Tell You About the Student's Thinking?

A picture *is* worth a thousand words. Students in the primary grades continue to develop number sense while working more with the concepts of addition and subtraction.

As they grow in their understanding of these operations and become more fluent in using addition and subtraction to solve a variety of problems, they begin to make generalizations that they can later apply when working with other operations such as multiplication and division. The following activity was conducted in Michel Wilson's first-grade math class and required students to apply their knowledge of doubles and addition as they worked through the problem, representing their solution with both pictures and numbers.

John is catching spiders. All spiders have 8 legs. John put 1 spider in a blue box. He put 1 spider in a red box. How many spider legs did he put in the two boxes?

To start the lesson, Mr. Wilson showed a short video clip of spiders followed by a lively discussion of who had seen spiders, who had spiders in their house, and who was afraid of spiders. The end result was that Mr. Wilson wanted to make sure his students knew that all spiders had eight legs. To reinforce this, students were given a plastic spider to keep on their desk, and he had students work in pairs so that they could tackle the problem together. Since the problem was somewhat easy, he had determined that the entire problem could be done in pairs instead of independently. The students had a number of other manipulatives and tools at their disposal such as two-color counters, color tiles, dry-erase boards, one sheet of easel paper with chart markers, and a calculator. Each group was allowed to choose the manipulatives they thought would help them the most.

With a solid start, the groups started to talk through the problem and draw pictures of the spiders that they had on their desk. Sean decided to divide his paper into two sections with each section representing one of the boxes, which he labeled blue and red. Once he had a spider in each box, he started to answer the questions at the bottom of the sheet. Mr. Wilson challenged all of his students to create a number sentence that described the number of legs in each box and then the number of spider legs in all. The students discovered that once they remembered to use doubles the problem became easier, and they realized that while some of them couldn't count by eights to find out the number of spider legs in the boxes, they could count by twos and keep track of their totals until they reached the number of legs. Mr. Wilson's efforts to get his students to begin seeing the situation not just as a picture with one answer but as a number sentence will help connect this process for students, and as he extends this problem to other situations the connection made here will aid students. This problem could be made more complex for students needing a greater challenge by increasing the number of boxes or the number of spiders in each box. The possibilities are endless.

Although Sean's work shows his understanding of how many legs are in the first box, he missed the mark with the second box and instead showed a sentence that represented the entire picture. (See Figure 3–2.)

Manipulatives are certainly one way to engage students in thinking about mathematics, and moving from the manipulative stage to the pictorial stage is a natural progression. Pictorial representations provide a more flexible strategy because students can choose how they want to draw a problem. One distinct advantage in allowing students to choose how they want to represent a problem is the thinking it reveals. That thinking may provide clues that some students are not developmentally where they might

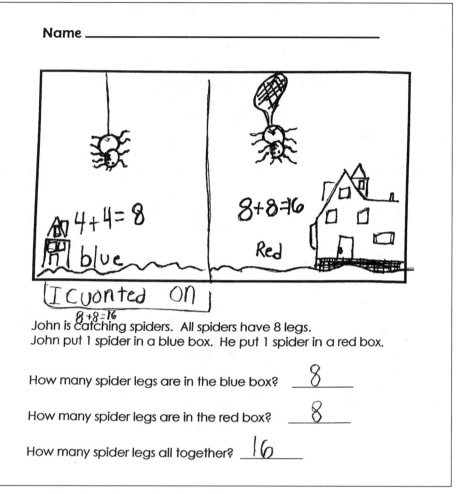

Figure 3–2 *Sean's work to solve the problem.*

need to be or where we think they are in their conceptual understanding. In other words, are they trying to solve multidigit computation by picturing the algorithm in their head, or are they trying to make some sense of the numbers that allows them to understand the math?

Have you ever watched in amazement as someone did multidigit computation all in their head? You can almost bet that they weren't solving a problem such as 345×598 by starting with 8×5. There was a lot more going on in their head than going through the steps of the traditional algorithm. Students will need to master the computational algorithm, but it is only one strategy. If we provide our students with only a single strategy for solving computation problems, we are shortchanging them. We need to provide them with classroom experiences that allow them to think about and solve computation problems in a variety of ways. By having students complete pages upon pages of "naked" math computation, you have no sense of their understanding of numbers. Just because students can complete these types of problems does not mean that they can make informed decisions about when to use certain types of computation. Using problems in context and allowing students to choose a representation that demonstrates their understanding of the math will provide much more information than pages of drill.

Place Value and Number Relationships

As students begin to conceptualize the size of numbers and their relationship to one another, it is important to provide opportunities for them to see conventional and nonconventional ways of representing the numbers. Again, they may not be able to generate many representations on their own, but they should have opportunities to identify them. Figure 3–3 shows several possible ways a student might begin to represent a number; in this case the number is 34. Using the concept formation strategy, students would be given a blank template with the number being represented and then an additional page that provides several choices that either were or were not represen-

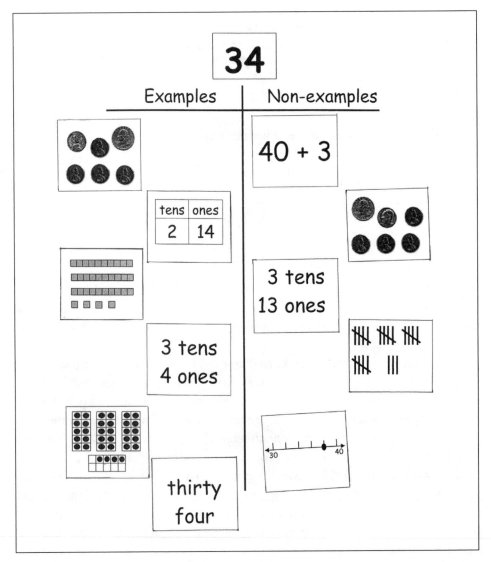

Figure 3–3 *Some ways to represent the number 34*

tations of 34. Based on their understanding of the concept, students would then place the picture or numbers in the correct column. By providing the students with several representations to choose from, some of which are alternate forms of the number, a teacher can get a sense of how well the student has conceptualized the concept. As students progress, they can be challenged to include their own representations. The same strategy could be applied to a variety of other concepts such as odd and even, skip counting, and patterns. The key is to provide many possible examples. Numbers such as 34 do not need to be represented as just 3 tens and 4 ones. Students should also recognize that 2 tens and 14 ones has the same value. At the same time other forms such as tally marks, coins, and ten frames can be used to describe the number.

Most students will start school with some sense of the relationship numbers have to one another, and some may even have developed an early awareness of the size of numbers. Here again, all students need opportunities to first see numbers being compared and then have opportunities to work with those number relationships. Figure 3–4 shows one example of how students might be encouraged to practice number relationships. Any theme will work; this example shows a series of three cookie jars. Each jar is labeled with one of the words *less, same,* or *more.* In this activity students are given a target number, and they are then asked to represent that number first with a manipulative and then with pictorial and number representations.

In Mrs. Dashiell's class she starts the activity using chocolate chip cookie cereal. As she announces the target number, students use the cookies to represent the same value in the center cookie jar. As the students check to see if they are correct, she directs them to next represent a number less than the target and then a number more than the target. Once the students have their manipulatives in place, she asks several of them to communicate their representations. Donnie tells her that since the number in the middle jar is 10 he put 2 cookies in the small jar and 12 cookies in the large

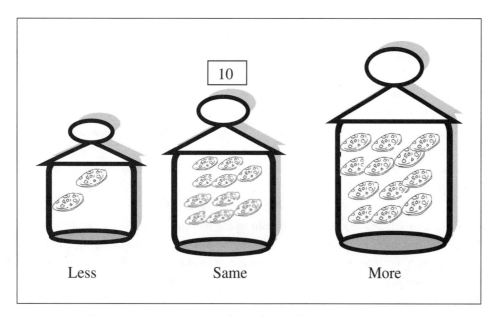

Figure 3–4 *One way to practice number relationships*

jar. It is important for students to verbalize the relationship of the numbers, so Mrs. Dashiell has each student that shares complete his or her sentence using the relationship of the numbers, not just the manipulatives. After students have shared their numbers, they are next directed to write the numeric representation for the values in each of the jars. Since she uses laminated pages, students can use dry- or wet-erase markers for their writing. This allows the pages to be reused for another activity. Mrs. Dashiell prompts them to complete the activity by drawing another picture that represents the same values in each of the jars. Students have now had an opportunity to relate the size of numbers to one another using a manipulative, a numeric representation, and another picture of their choice. Since the numbers were manageable, the manipulative worked well in this case. Students could also use a variety of other ways to represent their numbers such as dominoes, cards, or counters. Once the numbers increase in size, the cookie jars can become bean pots, or base ten blocks can be used as the manipulative.

Asking students to represent values that are two more or two less than a number or five more and five less can also provide information on their understanding of numbers and their relationship. This is an activity that could easily be used at a station using any type of manipulative and theme.

Computation and Representations

Students need the same opportunities when working with story problems. Mathematics is best learned by students when it is connected to the world around them. For that reason, story problems should be used as much as possible to connect the process to the context. Consider the following problem:

Micah bought 5 bags of candy from the store. If each bag contained 25 pieces of candy, how much candy in all did he buy?

Most students at this level would have no trouble completing this problem computationally using a traditional algorithm. The numbers are manageable and the computation easy, and we would be none the wiser as to what was really going on inside their heads. However, if we ask students to represent this problem pictorially, it is possible to see a little of what they are thinking. Figure 3–5 illustrates that two students may be at different stages in their conceptual understanding of whole-number computation and place value.

Both students drew a representation that correctly *matched* the problem, but you can begin to see the differences in the way each student thought about the mathematics. Student B seems to have already internalized a crucial concept: ten. By representing the problem using ten rods instead of the individual marks drawn by student A, student B demonstrated an understanding of place value and multiplication that allowed her a more sophisticated sense of the mathematics. While student A represented the problem as repeated addition in his drawing of each complete set, student B began to group like amounts by putting all of the tens together and all of the ones together and then multiplying a manageable benchmark number. Moving students away from counting as a method of computation and toward conceptualizing benchmark numbers such as ten allows students to transition to more complex computation. In this case, student A hadn't demonstrated that skill and needed additional practice with the base ten blocks and benchmark numbers such as ten and one hundred. While counting is certainly an early strategy for emerging learners, it is an inefficient method of solving computation problems, and students who continue to try to count when solving problems instead of chunking the numbers into meaningful quantities will experience more difficulty when the numbers become more complex.

You cannot see your students' thinking without occasionally having them represent problems pictorially. A representation strategy such as this can be used as an exit ticket or warm-up activity that will allow for a quick and easy informal assessment, providing valuable information. Here are some sample exit ticket problems using pictorial representations:

1. Margo baked cookies with her mom for the school bake sale. If they put 12 cookies on each pan, how many cookies did they bake in all if they used 5 pans?

2. Patty bought 5 bags of candy at the store. If each bag held 22 pieces of candy, how much candy did she have in all?

3. Charlie planted 5 rows of beans in his garden. If he planted 8 plants in each row, how many bean plants did he have in all?

4. There are 23 students in Mrs. Lemon's class and 24 students in Mrs. Deal's class. How many students were in the two classes in all?

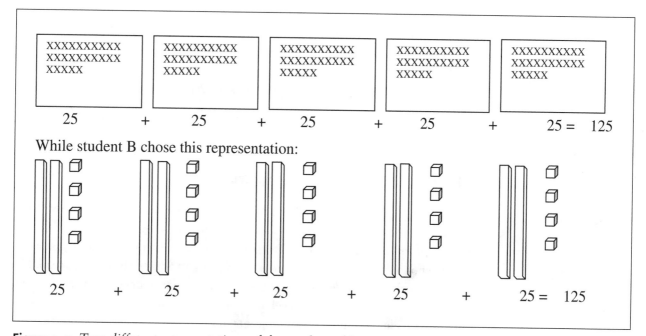

Figure 3–5 *Two different representations of the candy problem*

5. Trish had 53 books and Karen had 27 books. How many books did they have in all?

CLASSROOM-TESTED TIP

Exit tickets are great ways of assessing students' understanding of the daily lesson. By asking students to represent problems just before exiting the classroom and collecting their papers as they leave, you have a reliable method of assessment that can be used to inform the next day's instruction. These can also be used as warm-ups in the same way if you have your students complete them at the beginning of class. Having them do a quick check at the start of class provides you with some instant data on how students are progressing with a particular skill or concept. By doing this at the start of class, you can quickly look over their work and make decisions for that day's lesson or flexible grouping time.

Representing Fractions

Using manipulatives long enough for students to conceptualize some of the basic benchmark terms such as halves, thirds, and fourths is important, and it isn't enough for the teacher to model the fractions; the manipulatives need to be in students' hands. There, it has been said again: the manipulatives need to be in students' hands.

A number of commercially produced manipulatives can be used with fraction instruction. Pattern blocks are great for helping students see the relationship of part to whole. Using the yellow hexagon as the whole, students can clearly see that the red trapezoid is one-half of the whole while the blue rhombus is one-third. What happens when the trapezoid becomes the whole? What fraction does the triangle represent? Pattern blocks are useful in helping students see the relationships of part to whole.

However, as with many other concepts and processes in mathematics, manipulatives will go only so far in teaching about fractions. Keep in mind that the goal is to move students toward a more symbolic phase of representation, whether real or invented. It doesn't matter how the representation is drawn as long as it makes the math more meaningful for the student.

Take Your Cue from Reading Instruction

Look in any good reading manual and you will see a great deal of importance is placed on getting students ready to read. Building background knowledge is one of the key components in reading instruction. Its purpose is to increase the likelihood that a student will not only be interested in but also understand what he is about to read. It is no different with math. We need to actively build on what students already know and can do. Regardless of the grade level and content, activating prior knowledge is essential to bringing meaning to new concepts. Brain research indicates that when new information is being introduced, students are trying to connect it with what they already know. Isn't that how we all approach new knowledge? Many students do not see math around them on a daily basis, and unlike reading, they seldom go home at night and solve math problems for pleasure. They don't realize how math affects their lives, so it becomes important for us to find ways to make math meaningful to them and connect it to their world.

Before: Activate Prior Knowledge

Jump-start your students' thinking! Fractions are not just about pizza and dividing rectangles, and yet most of us learned fractions in that context. Before starting instruction on a new concept or skill, take the time to find out what the children already know about fractions and how they think about them. One way to do this is to engage students in a freewriting activity. It is more like a freewriting and drawing activity, but it allows students to demonstrate their understandings or misunderstandings where fractions are concerned. Students in Mrs. Churchman's second-grade class regularly engage in writing activities prior to learning new concepts and skills. Before the unit on fractions, she had them begin with a blank sheet of paper and she asked them to represent or describe as many fractional concepts and skills as they could. By encouraging students to use not only words and numbers but pictures and diagrams, she was able to see how some of them visualized the concepts. Seeing students use nonlinguistic forms of representations to illustrate fractional terms and processes can be very insightful for a classroom teacher. For example, one student in the class represented thirds, and while she divided a circle and a rectangle into three sections and shaded in one section, she didn't attempt to make the three parts appear equal. When vocabulary is present, the teacher needs to look for how it is used and in what context. Looking at student work, teachers need to ask questions such as these: "Are the students able to represent fractions not only as parts of a whole but also as parts of a set?" "Are there illustrations that represent numerators and denominators?" "Do the students have a beginning understanding of joining parts of fractions together?" The thinking and the prior knowledge that can be seen in student work of this nature is amazing.

Jump-starting their thinking might also mean finding unique and interesting applications for the concept. For example, Mrs. Churchman was able to use the Internet and the interactive white board to show her students some Egyptian history. As a way of getting students more interested in the upcoming unit on fractions, she showed students how the Egyptians represented fractions. To make the lesson more realistic, she had the students create papyrus scrolls for their work area as she presented an Egyptian math lesson. Mrs. Churchman explained that the Egyptians used only fractions with a numerator of one, called unit fractions. As Mrs. Churchman was showing students the fractions with the numerator of one, each of them was challenged to draw a picture that was shaded to represent each of the fractions.

During: On to the New Material

It is important to make sure students have multiple opportunities to see the benchmark fractions both as parts of a whole and as part of a set. Concept formation can also be used at this point to identify beginning fractional concepts and benchmarks. Using this strategy, the teacher provides students with an opportunity to build on what they already know about a specific topic while refining and clarifying the concept's specific characteristics. A chart similar to the one in Figure 3–6 is provided, and students are shown examples and nonexamples of the concept or skill you are trying to develop or extend (see CD for a blank chart). At the same time, it is important to make a conscious effort to avoid calling that concept by name. The purpose of this activity is to get students to describe, not name, the concept or skill.

Figure 3–6 is an example of one of the benchmark fractions, one-fourth. In this case we are representing the fraction as both a fractional part of a set and a fractional part of a whole. Depending on where students are in their skill development, examples might need to be limited to one or the other. As students study the chart and the examples, ask key questions such as, "What do the examples have in common?" and "How do the nonexamples differ?" As students respond, encourage them to describe the characteristics of the examples and at the same time be specific about why the nonexamples are nonexamples. One sample student response might be "In the top row, each column has one smiley face shaded in, but the example has four faces and the nonexample has only three faces." Allow students to continue verbalizing the characteristics, and when they think they know what the concept is, prompt them to create their own examples and nonexamples. A note of caution: Make sure students aren't just drawing a different shape and mimicking each example in quantity and shading. Not all students will be as quick to reach a conclusion about the concept as others. For that reason, having students draw their own examples allows them to continue to be engaged while giving the rest of the students additional time to continue thinking about the similarities and differences found in the examples and nonexamples.

For students in grades preK–2, this particular concept may or may not already be a part of their working knowledge. For that reason, it is important to take time to activate all prior knowledge no matter what the skill is by using key questions to get students thinking about a specific topic. You never know what misconceptions might be uncovered. Occasional informal assessments such as this activity work great with dry-erase boards as a quick check or as a precursor to introducing equivalent or more complex fractions and mixed numbers.

Examples	**Nonexamples**
☼ ☼ ☼ ☼	☼ ☼
☺ ☺ ☺ ☺	☺ ☺ ☺
▭	▭
♡ ♡ ♡ ♡	♡ ♡ ♡ ♡ ♡

Figure 3–6 *Chart used for concept formation*

We can also activate prior knowledge using manipulatives. In Chapter 2, we described how to use two-color counters to help develop the concept of fractional parts of a set where the whole was represented by the total number of counters and each color became a part of the set. Activities such as this help students model the concepts, but unless your classroom has an unlimited budget for manipulatives (and mine doesn't), you have to move from the concrete manipulative to student representations to continue to illustrate this concept. In essence you are building the bridge that will connect the concrete to the symbolic representation. It also allows for more flexibility when you have your students draw something other than counters or tiles.

CLASSROOM-TESTED TIP

In Mrs. Elwood's class, students use a washcloth as their manipulative mat. As they are rolling their dice or working with two-color counters, the washcloth serves two different purposes, the first is noise suppression. The washcloth helps to cut down on the sounds made when the dice roll or counters are dropped to the table. The other advantage of using washcloths is that it helps to keep the manipulatives on the desk instead of rolling around on the floor. As the washcloths get dirty, she just takes them home for a good washing and brings them back the next day.

After: Been There, Done That—Moving On!

Don't you just love it when a student says, "Why are we doing this? We learned that in the last chapter," and "We've already taken the test," or "Why are we doing a geometry problem when we are supposed to be working on addition?" Like it or not that is how most students view mathematics instruction: in isolation. It becomes imperative to continue to spiral back and reassess student thinking as well as help students make connections to the new concepts as we are teaching them. We need to provide students with opportunities to demonstrate the connective nature of mathematics and extend and refine their thinking as it relates to the more complex processes. One of the easiest ways to spiral back on content is to use an exit or entry ticket that combines concepts already taught. Give students a problem or group of problems to solve, and as they leave the room they hand you their exit ticket. If you are using entry tickets, they give them to you as they arrive for class. Entry and exit tickets can provide wonderful information on what concepts are being retained and what concepts need some reteaching.

The Role of the Teacher

It is important for teachers to provide students with multiple opportunities to interact with concepts and express themselves mathematically so that their thinking is revealed. It doesn't come from pages of drill and kill, and it doesn't come from limiting them to

Figure 3–7 *Using a dry-erase board, these students have an opportunity to represent their thinking.*

one numeric representation. Studies such as TIMSS (Trends in International Mathematics and Science Study) illustrate the need for a change in our approach to mathematics instruction. One such change is in allowing students to work through problem-solving situations either independently or cooperatively and construct meaning from the mathematics without having to be told what math is involved (Figure 3–7). Students who are allowed to work through problems without first having to memorize steps in an algorithm are much more likely to internalize the mathematics and thus reduce the nearly 53 percent of time spent reviewing concepts in an average eighth-grade classroom (Hiebert et al. 2003).

A mathematics class rich in context and problem-solving opportunities is much more likely to yield students ready for more complex situations, and allowing students to use their own representations to illustrate their thinking will help teachers immediately zero in on misconceptions and inefficient strategies.

Questions for Discussion

1. How can a standards-based classroom be a problem-based classroom?

2. How can the use of representations help students extend and refine their understanding of mathematics?

3. What connections to the context can students demonstrate with their representations?

4. How can teachers use alternative forms of representations to help jumpstart instruction?

4

Using Numbers and Symbols to Represent Mathematical Ideas

Like other forms of written literacy, mathematical representations allow for visual inspection of work and reduce cognitive demands on memory.

—Sara P. Fisher and Christopher Hartmann, "Math through the Mind's Eye"

Moving from Pictures to Equations

As we discussed in Chapter 3, pictures are an important way for children to learn to show their mathematical thinking, and the sophistication of their pictorial representations grows developmentally. The leap between pictures and numbers, however, is not an easy one for some students. Moving from the concrete to the abstract requires a deep understanding of a topic, although we might argue that there are plenty of students who can use numbers successfully without having worked in the concrete first. However, when we ask them to explain their thinking in words, or even to go from the abstract of numbers to creating a concrete model of the process they used, we find that there are holes in their understanding and that they are often performing certain procedures automatically without a foundation of real understanding about why those procedures work or what they mean. Our goal, then, is to move students from pictures to equations when they are developmentally ready and to guide them toward more standard numerical representations when appropriate.

In this chapter, we discuss the importance of developing students' understanding of what numbers and symbols mean, and ways in which we can support them in this growth. We also discuss the role of invented algorithms and the use of equations to solve problems and visualize math ideas. Finally, the role of the teacher in this area of student learning is examined.

It's All About Timing

Timing is everything, as they say. If we attempt to move our students from the concrete to the abstract too early, or worse yet, skip the concrete altogether, we'll find ourselves with a group of students who are consumed with remembering formulas and facts without really thinking about the mathematics behind a problem. If they can't recall those algorithms, they'll have absolutely nothing to fall back on. We do a disservice to students when we teach procedures rather than concepts. How many of us learned that the formula for the area of a rectangle is length times width? It's likely that we stored this procedural approach to an area problem in our brain and retrieved it when we thought it was applicable, without creating a visual in our head or on paper that would assist in our understanding of the problem. Similarly, we may have the formula for the perimeter of a rectangle tucked safely away: $2s^1 + 2s^2$. How many times, though, have we seen a student faced with a perimeter problem of an irregular polygon who did not use the understanding that perimeter is the distance *around* something? Rather, the student tried to apply the formula for a rectangle to the irregular polygon and froze up when it did not work. The student had nothing to fall back on, no mental tool box from which to pull different strategies.

What do numbers really mean? How can we support students' growing understanding of numbers and symbols? These are important questions that we must ask ourselves as we plan meaningful learning experiences for our students. Defining the word *number* is not an easy task in itself. Indeed, one Web inquiry into the definition of the word led us to more than ten separate definitions! It is no wonder that without concrete learning experiences some students find conventions such as numbers and symbols very difficult to master.

Two concepts that are introduced in the primary grades are addition and subtraction. Fortunately, the days of simply requiring students to memorize the facts without connecting them to some type of model are behind us. Real understanding of these concepts is developed through manipulating objects in and out of groups before the numbers and symbols associated with the task are ever introduced. In fact, the language we use typically does not follow the symbols in the beginning. We are more likely to say, "How can we show four and three more?" rather than ask students what four plus three equals. One way we can help our students to make the connection between the concrete and the abstract is by using manipulatives, linking the process to numbers and symbols, and then weaning them from the manipulatives. In the following task, students are asked to solve a "join change unknown" problem.

Jenny has six crayons. Maria also has some crayons. Together they have thirteen crayons. How many does Maria have?

This task is a little more challenging than many story problems because in it there is an unknown piece that, together with the given amount of six crayons, gives a total of thirteen crayons. Many students assumed the problem involved combining amounts because the word "together" is in the story. However, there was confusion about what exactly was being combined. Several students counted out six crayons and thirteen crayons and then incorrectly combined the two quantities given for a total of nineteen crayons. When asked if that solution made sense, they reread the problem and realized that their answer couldn't be right because *together* they have thirteen crayons.

If students have a manipulative such as crayons, they can solve this problem in more than one way. In Figure 4–1 we see one student's record of how he approached the problem. David counted out thirteen crayons and then took away, or crossed off, six (representing Jenny's share), leaving seven crayons, which represented Maria's share. David used subtraction to solve this problem, taking a known part from a whole, leaving the remaining unknown part. Another student, Ji-Yung, used her fingers to solve the problem, as seen in Figure 4–2. She counted on from six crayons until she got to thirteen, putting a finger up to represent each additional crayon, and then counted how many fingers she had put up to get to thirteen. Ji-Yung used an addition model to solve the problem.

Figure 4–1 *David solved the problem using subtraction.*

Name_____

Jenny has 6 crayons. Maria also has some crayons. Together they have 13 crayons. How many does Maria have? _____7_____

Show how you solved this problem.

Figure 4–2 *Ji-Yung used addition to solve the problem.*

From each student's representations, we can make some assumptions about their mathematical understandings and their progression from concrete to pictorial to symbolic representations. First, it seems that both students understood what the problem was asking. In David's work, we can assume that he has one-to-one correspondence because he drew the known total of thirteen crayons and correctly crossed off the known quantity of six; he is comfortable making simple pictorial representations of the crayons he used to solve the problem; and he understood that the remaining seven crayons represented Maria's share, as evidenced by the number 7 written in the answer space. At first glance, we might assume from Ji-Yung's work that she simply uses her fingers to count. However, we can learn much more by studying her representation: she can write numbers in order from seven to thirteen; she is comfortable using a counting on strategy, and she knows where to *start* and *end* when using this strategy; and she understood that each finger she put up represented one of Maria's crayons, which she counted up at the end for a total of seven crayons.

By asking students to create a written representation of their thought processes when solving a problem, we are given a record that can be studied and revisited to check for mathematical understandings, strategies used, and compared against later work samples for evidence of growth.

David does not incorporate any numerical symbols in his work, other than to indicate the answer, but Ji-Yung does use numbers. Neither student attempts to assign any sort of equation to their process, indicating that they may not be developmentally ready to do so. However, given the understandings evidenced in their representations, it would be reasonable to assume that each of these students may be ready to see a more symbolic representation of how they solved their problem in the form of numbers, even if they are not ready to assign those symbols independently.

Figure 4–3 shows us a student making the connection between the numerical symbol and the quantity described by that number. She was given the task of turning over a number card, one at a time, and creating a tower with that many blocks. As we can learn from her representation, she understands what each number represents, she has one-to-one correspondence, and as a bonus, we can see that she can create a repeating pattern! This "simple" independent activity gives us some important information about her mathematical understandings, which can help to inform our instruction. For example, a learning goal for this student might be to generate the written number herself and create a tower with that many blocks, or combine numbers and towers to create new quantities. We might also push her growth in the area of patterns and ask her how she could describe her pattern using letters, or ask her if she could create a different kind of pattern.

Figure 4–3 *Making the connection between the numerical symbol and the quantity described by that number*

CLASSROOM-TESTED TIP

Use dot cards to help students begin to make the connection between the number symbol and a given quantity. Each card should have a dot arrangement as it looks on a domino, along with the number describing the quantity. These cards can be placed at centers, and students can pick a card and then create a tower out of Unifix cubes that matches the quantity and number shown on the card. Students can also take collections, such as beads, small plastic bugs, cotton balls, colorful foam-shape cutouts, or any other inviting material, and count them out into the quantities indicated on the dot cards. Students who are ready can create a pictorial representation of their work in their math journal.

In the following task, we can see two students' approaches to a problem. The record they created of their work gives us some insight into their facility with using the numeric symbols to represent their thinking. Here is the problem:

What is 10 doubled? How can this help you to figure out what 11 doubled is?

In Figure 4–4 we see how these students approached this problem. Joseph drew pictures to represent his thinking. He first drew two groups of ten flags each, showing twenty, and then drew two groups of eleven books each, showing twenty-two. It was unclear how he was making the connection between ten doubled and eleven doubled, so his teacher asked him to explain his thinking out loud. She wrote what he dictated

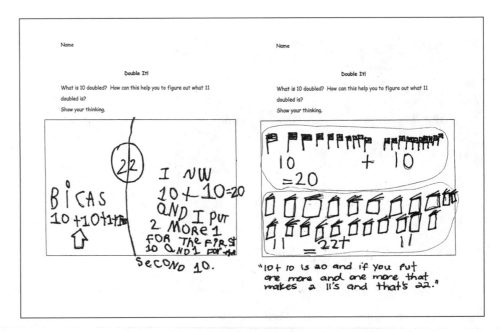

Figure 4–4 *Rami (*left*) and Joseph (*right*) each show their work to solve the same problem.*

under his work: "Ten plus ten is twenty, and if you put one more and one more that makes two elevens, and that's twenty-two." It was easy to see by his explanation that he was thinking of adding one to each of the two groups of ten to represent eleven doubled. We can also see in his work that he is comfortable using numbers to describe a quantity and can use the addition and equal symbols to represent an equation. Joseph is comfortable using pictures as a model, so he showed as much as he could through pictures and then explained the rest orally to his teacher.

Rami thought about this problem numerically from the beginning. He envisioned doubling ten as ten plus ten, and then added one to each ten to represent eleven doubled, and he showed it all through numbers and words. By comparing the two work samples, we can see two different levels of facility with numbers that we might encounter in a primary class. Each student understands that doubling a quantity means making two groups of it, and each has a preferred method of representing the concept, both of which incorporate numbers in some way.

The Role of Alternative Algorithms

Alternative, or invented, algorithms are procedures children have invented to help them solve mathematical problems. They are termed *alternative* because they are often idiosyncratic and do not resemble the algorithms that are traditionally associated with operations. *Principles and Standards for School Mathematics* (NCTM 2000) asserts the importance of encouraging students to use written mathematical representations to help them make sense, even if those representations are unconventional. For example, the traditional way of solving a two-digit addition problem involves "putting down and carrying," or regrouping, as it is commonly termed. A child using an alternative algorithm might use an expanded form to add, as shown in Figure 4–5.

We find that in many instances in which students are using a traditional algorithm to solve an addition or subtraction problem, they are doing so without a strong understanding of why the procedure works or even what it means. They are simply following steps that they have been taught for solving similar problems.

In Figure 4–6, we see how one student solved the same addition problem (65 + 27) in different ways. The first method she chose was using an expanded form of the numbers. She rewrote the numbers as tens and ones, and then added the tens first and then added the ones and combined her partial sums. This method requires an understanding of place value and the ability to decompose and recompose numbers. In the second solution, she decomposed the second addend into friendlier numbers—20 + 5 + 2 (27)—and added each of these parts in turn, starting with the decade (20). Again,

Traditional Algorithm	Alternative Algorithm
^{1}27	27 = 20 + 7
+68	+68 = 60 + 8
95	80 + 15 = 95

Figure 4–5 *Traditional and alternative approaches to solving an addition problem*

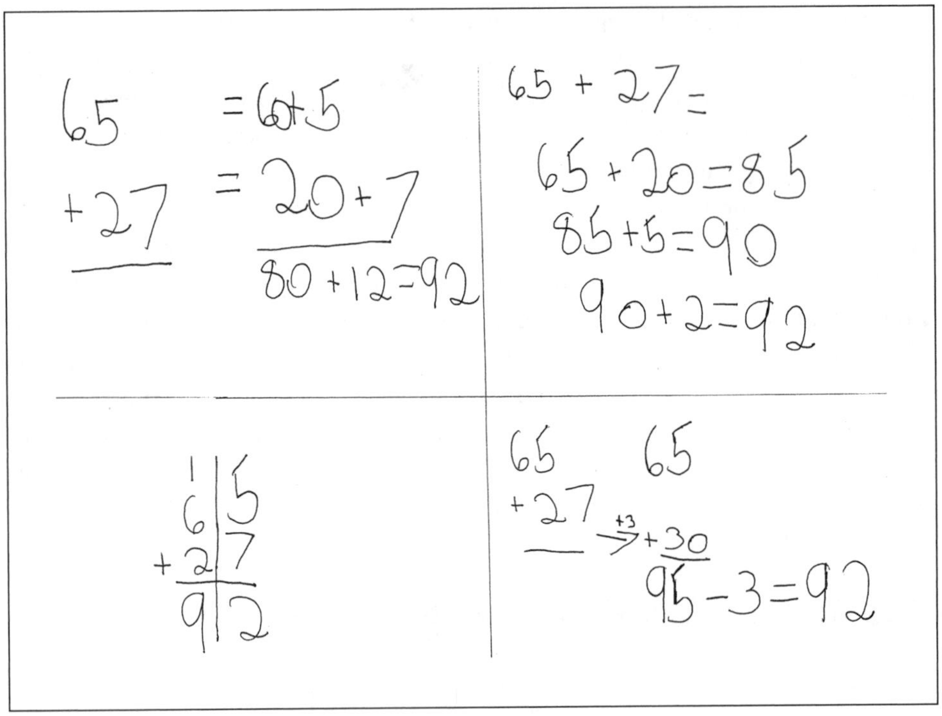

Figure 4–6 *One student solving the same addition problem four different ways*

an ability to decompose numbers is required in this approach, along with some kind of organization (either on paper or mentally) to keep track of the parts added. The third way she solved the problem was by using the traditional algorithm. While she could solve the problem correctly using this method, we don't gain any insight into her understanding of numbers or the concept of addition by looking at that solution. For all we can tell, she has memorized a procedure and applied it. Finally, she solves the problem using a compensation strategy. She added three to the addend twenty-seven to make it a friendlier number to work with, and then she took the three back out after she added sixty-five and thirty together. This student has many strategies from which she can choose when solving similar problems.

Subtraction also lends itself to the creation of alternate algorithms. Traditionally, students are taught to subtract the ones first, and if the ones quantity on top is smaller than the ones quantity on the bottom, they must "borrow" from the tens and give to the ones to make the ones quantity on the top larger. They then proceed through the problem from right to left in the same fashion. There are probably very few among us who have not seen some students stumble over these steps time and time again. This is especially true when subtracting across zeroes, as in the problem 104 – 58. Students using the traditional algorithm are required to "cross out" and "borrow" multiples times, and if a student leaves out one of those regroupings, the solution is wrong and they very often cannot figure out why. Imagine what will happen when they get to much larger numbers with multiple zeroes in them! Students who are more flexible in their thinking and who are given the opportunity to invent their own procedure for a problem will do so in a way that makes sense to them. In Figure 4–7 we see how two students approached the same subtraction problem (203 – 95) using different strategies. In the first problem, it is evident that the student used the traditional algorithm to solve the problem. She started from the right and decided she could not subtract three minus nine, so she went to the tens, but there were no tens to borrow from, so she kept going to the hundreds. However, her confusion with this procedure is evident because, while she took "one" from the hundreds, she did not remember that she must give it to the tens and then borrow again, taking one of those tens to give to the ones. Her solution is wrong because she failed to follow the procedure correctly. In the second student's work, we see a more unconventional way of subtracting. This student added five to the second number, making it one hundred, a much friendlier number to work with. She then added the same quantity to the first number, making it 208. She kept the *distance* between the two numbers the same. These numbers could then be subtracted mentally ("208 go back 100 is 108"). There was no regrouping involved or steps to remember. The second student exhibited a fundamental understanding of the concept of subtraction: that the difference between two numbers is the distance between them, and if we keep the distance the same, then we can adjust the numbers to more friendly ones to work with. As these examples show us, alternative, or invented, algorithms often give us great insight into a child's understanding (or misunderstanding) and thinking about a problem.

As students begin to make the connection that they can use the inverse of subtraction, or addition, to solve what we would traditionally label as a subtraction problem, we see some exciting mathematical thinking and approaches to problems. For example, if a student was presented with the problem in the example above (203 − 95), he might jump from 95 to 100 (+5), then from 100 to 200 (+100), then from 200 to 203 (+3) and add up all his jumps.

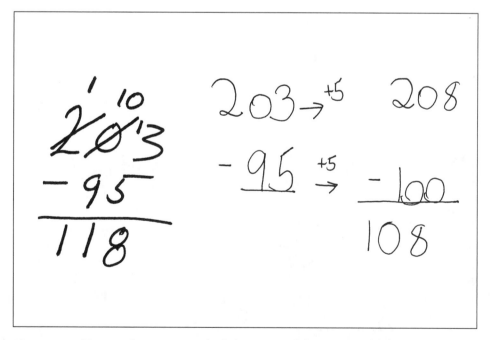

Figure 4–7 *Two students approached the same subtraction problem using different strategies.*

We can see in Figure 4–8 that Kaylie used, among other strategies, this open number line model to solve a problem. She was trying to find the difference between nineteen and forty-three, so she jumped from nineteen to the closest decade (twenty), then from twenty to thirty to forty, and then from forty to forty-three. She recorded her jumps and then added them up. This demonstrates a counting up strategy to solve a subtraction problem. We can see in Kaylie's work that she is comfortable using numbers to represent her thinking and that decades are friendly numbers on which she relies to help her solve a problem. What a great resource she now has in this representation to share her thinking with her peers.

The wonderful thing about alternative algorithms is that they develop out of a student's growing understanding of a concept, without having conventions and rules applied to them. These invented approaches to solving problems provide us, their teachers, with great insight into students' understanding of a concept, their confidence as mathematicians, and their development as independent thinkers. It is so exciting to see a student solve a problem in a way we never thought of! We need to encourage our students to solve mathematical problems in ways that make sense to them, so that they are thinking and reasoning about numbers. Students who solve addition problems

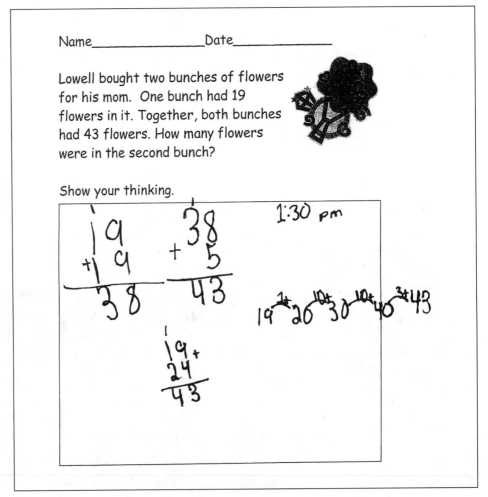

Figure 4–8 *Kaylie used an open number line model to solve this problem.*

only by counting on their fingers, or by drawing a picture, may eventually need to be exposed to and guided toward more efficient strategies. That is not to say that we should dismiss their approach to solving a problem; rather, by exposing them to and discussing the ways other students solve problems, we can coach them to the next level.

CLASSROOM-TESTED TIP

Let problem solving be a primary element in your mathematics instruction. Present the children with a rich math story to solve and observe the strategies they use to solve it. While the students are working, make a note of the students who use efficient and understandable strategies to solve the problem and have them share with the whole class at the end of the math lesson. Ask a student to explain in his or her own words, or paraphrase, how a classmate solved a problem.

Using Equations to Solve Problems and Visualize Ideas

As mentioned previously, we do a great disservice to our students when we teach procedures and algorithms without letting students develop their own understanding of a concept. However, we would be negligent as well if we did not help students make the connection between ideas and equations and see how equations can help us solve problems and visualize ideas.

An equation represents a whole idea. For example, $4 + 6 = 10$. In order for this equation to have meaning for students, other than as a memorized fact, they must understand several things. First, they have to understand what 4, 6, and 10 mean (they represent different-sized quantities), and, perhaps more important, they must understand what the equals sign represents. The notion that the equals sign balances an equation is essential. Here is one experience a second-grade teacher had when assessing her students' understanding of this concept:

TEACHER: I am going to write an equation on the interactive white board, and I want you give me your thoughts. (*She writes 12 = 5 + 7*)
SHERI: You can't write it like that.
TEACHER: No? Why not?
SHERI: Because the answer has to come last, and twelve is the answer.
TEACHER: OK. What does this symbol mean (*pointing to the equals sign*)?
RICHY: It means the answer. Like, if I had the problem five plus five equals ten, the equals sign tells you that the answer is next, which is ten.
TEACHER: Does anyone else have any thoughts?
CAROLINE: I think the answer can come first, because five plus seven equals twelve, so that's just like saying twelve equals twelve.
TEACHER: Caroline, can you use counters on the board here to show us what that looks like? (*Caroline stamps out a set of twelve counters, and arranges them under*

the number twelve, and then stamps out a set of five counters, arranging them under the number five, and finally stamps out a set of seven counters, arranging them under the number seven.)

TEACHER: Aidan, what has Caroline done here?

AIDAN: She put twelve counters on the side with the twelve and five counters and seven counters on the side with the five and the seven.

TEACHER: How many counters are on each side of the equals sign?

Aidan: There are twelve on that side and twelve on the other side.

TEACHER: It sounds like Caroline and Aidan have noticed something about what's on each side of the equals sign. Let's look at this math sentence. (*She writes on the board 3 + 4 = 4 + 3*) Would someone like to come up and show us what this might look like with counters? (*Tyler approaches the board and stamps out seven counters under each part of the equation.*)

TEACHER: Tyler, can you explain what you just did?

TYLER: Well, three plus four equals seven, and four plus three equals seven, so I put seven counters on each side. Both sides show the same thing.

TEACHER: Let's try one more. (*She writes 10 − 2 = 4 + 4*) Is this true?

MACKENZIE: Yes, it's true because ten take away two equals eight, and four plus four equals eight, so both sides of the equals sign equal eight.

TEACHER: What, then, does the equals sign mean?

SHERI: It means that whatever is on one side of the equals sign must be as much as what's on the other side of it.

TEACHER: Exactly. The equals sign balances what's on each side. They must be equal in value, even if they don't look the same. That's why you can write twelve equals five plus seven, because each side of the equation is the same amount. In your math journal, write a math sentence or draw a picture to show what the equals sign means.

This conversation highlights a misconception that must be cleared up before equations have real meaning for students. Certainly, without this fundamental understanding of what the equals sign represents, students will struggle with algebraic concepts and higher math. By simply assessing students' understanding of this concept through informal conversation and then asking them to process what they've learned through journal writing, we can help to ensure that they master this very important concept.

Once we are comfortable that our students understand what an equation is, including what its parts represent, and that they have constructed their own knowledge and understanding about a concept, we can begin to introduce symbols and equations associated with certain concepts. For example, in the primary grades we talk about putting groups together and counting the total. We do this over and over with manipulatives before we introduce the symbols + and =. However, once students fully understand that when we put groups together we are adding, they can rely on using those symbols to create equations associated with that action.

Numbers and symbols also serve to reduce the cognitive demands on the learner. For example, when working to solve a complex problem, students can use numbers and symbols to record intermediary steps without having to remember them. They can then refer back to the notes they made when they need them.

The Role of the Teacher

In the area of numbers and symbols, the teacher acts as a coach, paying careful attention to the moment when a student is ready to move from concrete representations to more abstract ones. For us to be able to do this, we must provide our students with many opportunities to show what they understand about a topic, through manipulatives, paper representations, and verbal explanations. Students also must be exposed to different ways of solving problems so they can compare their strategies with others and refine theirs to an efficient, meaningful strategy upon which they can draw in the future. Equations help to form complete pictures and explain actions through symbols. For example, the equation $25 - 13 = $ ____ means the quantity twenty-five less the quantity thirteen. Allowing students to use the shortcut of symbols and equations must not be the result of shortcutting them through the process of developing their own understanding of mathematical concepts and ideas. The time we spend in concept development, assessment, and determining the right moment at which to introduce numbers and symbols is time well invested and will help to develop competent, confident young mathematicians.

One of the most important roles of the mathematics teacher is requiring students to justify their thinking. It is not enough for students simply to give an answer. We must challenge them to defend the strategy they chose to solve a problem and to prove that they are right. Questions we might ask to do this include the following:

■ How did you solve this problem?

■ Why did you choose that strategy?

■ Why do you think you're right?

■ How else could you have solved it?

By pushing our students to think beyond just getting the right answer, we are helping them to think more deeply about the mathematics they are learning.

CLASSROOM-TESTED TIP

Helping students gain flexibility and fluency in mathematical thinking should be one of the goals of any math program. There are many ways in which we can help our students to develop these skills. Try these activities out as warm-ups, sponges (time fillers), or homework activities.

■ *Renaming a Number:* Help students to think about different ways we can name numbers. For example: $56 = 50 + 6$ or $25 + 25 + 6$ or $10 + 10 + 10 + 10 + 10 + 6$, and so on.

■ *Target Number:* This activity is similar to renaming a number. You select a target number and students must think of as many possible ways to reach the target number as they can. For example, 12 can be reached by adding 10 + 2 or by doubling 6.

■ *Who Am I?* Students are given clues about numbers and must guess the number. For example, "I am a number between ten and twenty and I have a seven in my ones place" (seventeen). Students can generate their own "Who Am I?" riddles.

■ *Buzz:* Students gather in a circle. A number is selected, such as two, and as the students count off starting at one, those students who would say a multiple of two instead say, "Buzz" (e.g., one, buzz, three, buzz, five, buzz, seven, buzz, and so on).

■ *Predict Then Count:* The group gathers in a circle and counts off by ones. The leader then selects a value to count by (such as two), and before counting students can predict what they think will be the last number announced. For example, if there are nine children in the group and they are counting by two each time, students might predict that twenty will be the last number announced, or some may correctly predict that eighteen will be the last number. While the children are counting, record the numbers they announce on chart paper. After counting, discuss how the predictions compared with the actual number, solicit strategies for how students figured it out, and look for patterns in the chart.

■ *What's the Question?* Give students an answer, such as "The answer is ten. What's the question?" Student responses might be "How much is a dime?" or "How many fingers do I have?" and so on.

■ *Starting Where?* Ask students to count by ones, for example, and they respond by asking you, "Starting where?" Choose different numbers to start with, such as "Count by ones starting at nineteen." Get them to count over landmark numbers, such as one hundred, to build their fluency with larger numbers as well.

Questions for Discussion

1. How can we help students make the connection between concrete representations and symbolic ones?

2. What is the value of alternative or invented algorithms?

3. How can we ensure our students have a deep understanding of a concept before moving them to symbolic representations?

4. What is the value in asking students to justify their thinking?

5. What is the role of the teacher in introducing numbers and symbols to students?

5

Using Tables and Graphs to Record, Organize, and Communicate Ideas

But I Already Found One Answer!

When presented with problems that offer multiple solutions or problems that ask students to find a pattern in their solution, many students are confused as to how best to organize their information. Many are still at a stage wherein drawing pictures is the most efficient strategy, and they aren't quite sure how to create tables that make their work more organized. Providing students with situations in which they can keep track of solutions in a table and helping them set up that table will help develop their problem-solving skills. As students begin to see the relationship between the pictures and the information found on the tables, their proficiency in using this strategy will improve.

In Mrs. Lemon's second-grade classroom the students are just discovering the advantages tables can provide. She presents her class with the following problem:

Lindsey bought 5 pencils from the store. If each pencil costs 10¢, how much did she spend?

Mrs. Lemon directs her students to set their table up by starting with what they know about the numbers in the problem. One of the concepts she needed to get across to students was the idea of unit cost. Most of the students were ready to set their table up in such a way as to assign the cost of 10¢ to 5 pencils. This is a common error when students are at this level. She had them reread the problem and then showed them how to set up their table instead of drawing a picture or writing a number sentence, which most of them had already done! The students were prompted to look at the numbers in the table and first see whether they could determine how much the five pencils would cost and then extend to the next level and see how much six pencils cost. Although this problem looks simplistic, it is really complex. Students are looking at a function table, patterns, counting by tens, and with Mrs. Lemon's careful guidance, they can extend this table on to higher values. Figure 5–1 illustrates the type of table she used.

1 pencil	2 pencils	3 pencils	4 pencils	5 pencils
10 cents	20 cents	30 cents	40 cents	?

Figure 5–1 *Using a table to help solve a problem*

It takes a lot of practice, but primary students can learn to set up their own tables to solve problems like this. Some additional problems that can be solved using a table include the following:

1. **Burt has 4 boxes of books. Each box has 12 books. How many books are in 4 boxes?**

2. **Maria's mother baked cookies. Each tray holds 8 cookies. How many cookies are on 5 trays?**

3. **If there are 50 pages in a notebook, how many pages are there in 5 notebooks?**

4. **If 7 boys each have 2 pair of shoes, how many pair of shoes are there altogether?**

It's All About Me!

Students at the primary level should be given opportunities to experience graphing situations that are all about themselves and the world around them. The colors of shirts, types of shoes, number of family members, and pets or no pets can all be topics for the primary graph. Understanding how these data are gathered and deciding what they mean is essential to knowing why graphic representations are important. Primary students may not yet be aware of all the types of graphs they can create. Pictographs, bar graphs, real graphs, and tally charts should be familiar territory, but deciding which one to use or how to set up that graph is unfamiliar territory at this point. Modeling all of the various displays and reinforcing what they mean will help conceptualize these data representations. Students need to understand that what they are graphing helps determine how they will graph the information, and that some displays are just not appropriate for certain data types. In this chapter, we look at some ways to incorporate a variety of graphing displays and at the analysis that needs to take place once the graphing is complete.

Why Graph?

Are we asking students to graph for the sake of graphing, or are we asking them to graph in order to answer a legitimate question? The purpose of graphing is to organize data in a meaningful display to make analysis easier. The purpose of collecting data is to answer a question or questions. According to NCTM (2000, 108), students at this grade level need to "formulate questions that can be addressed with data and collect, organize, and display relevant data to answer them." Data isn't a set of disconnected numbers used solely to practice finding mean, median, and mode. Data is information gathered in an attempt to see a trend, solve a problem, or support a hypothesis. Students in kindergarten through grade 2 have a lot of interests that can be tapped for the purposes of learning about statistical displays, but far too often they are limited to working with a meaningless set of numbers. When this happens, no knowledge can be gained concerning the appropriate selection of the statistical display, and no knowledge is gained concerning the information the graph reveals beyond the arbitrary numbers used. Imagine the excitement that can be generated when students begin to see statistical representations about themselves or about topics of interest to them. When students have a stake in the data and an interest in the question being investigated, their analysis of the data becomes so much more than a series of numbers generated to find measures of central tendency. The standards-based classroom may at times seem limited in the type of graphing display that is promoted at a given grade level. Students in grades K–2 should engage in the creation and analysis of several different types of data displays. Two important things should be kept in mind: (1) once a graph has been taught, it should continue to be used and continue to be a choice when students are determining the most appropriate display to represent their data, and as always, (2) students need to begin with the concrete and move toward symbolic representation of the data.

From Real Graphs to Pictographs

Ask any primary teacher about their graphing activities and they will begin with a description of the real graphs created in the classroom. A real graph uses actual objects in the representation. For example, the teacher might ask a question concerning the types of shoes students are wearing. The comparison might be made between those students wearing shoes that tie versus those that don't or between the colors of shoes. Students would then create a graph using their shoes, and then with one shoe on and one shoe off, students would discuss the display in front of them. By the time students reach second grade, you may have a hard time convincing them to take off their shoes to create a graph, and even if you do convince them, you need to be prepared for the choruses of "phew" as shoes are removed. It's going to happen! Students can create real graphs using buttons, sorting cubes, or other manipulatives on hand. Students themselves can become part of a real graph. Having students stand as if they were the information to be graphed is another way of getting them up and moving but also experiencing the process of putting together a graph.

An alternative to real graphs, but a natural progression, is the pictograph, and like the real graph, the pictograph does not need to be on a numeric scale. Generally, pictographs with a scale can be used to help students practice skip counting, using the scale to represent the quantities being graphed. Using pictures or representations of the objects in the graph instead of the real thing provides a little more flexibility in what we can graph. Take time, however, to help students connect the two types of graphs. It may not be obvious to all students that the two data displays are related. For the data to be meaningful and easier to graph, limit the comparisons you ask students to make within the data to three to five categories. If the number of categories is much larger, it will be more difficult to answer the question that the graph is supposed to address.

Data can come from a variety of sources. Students love taking and giving surveys, which provides a wealth of information suitable for graphing. For example, one favorite topic to address with pictographs is the type of pets students have or would like to have. Adding the "would like to have" category provides an opportunity for students without pets to participate. Another option would be to have a category of no pets. Students could bring in pictures of their pets, draw pictures of their pets, or cut pictures out of a magazine of a favorite type of pet. Trying to graph all of the different types of pets could create too many categories, and some categories might have only one or two pets. Instead, why not create specific categories that allow your students to put different animals in like categories, such as pets with fur, pets without fur, pets with two legs, pets with four legs, pets that walk, pets that fly, or pets that slither? Students can imagine seeing their pets on the graphs as they put pictures on the graph. Another option is to take advantage of the die cuts that most schools have available and use the shapes to represent the animals or objects to be graphed. Most craft stores now stock tubs of foam shapes that come in all sizes and themes. These shapes make wonderful graphs, and they can be reused again and again for a variety of graphing activities.

Students should also be using tally marks to keep track of the data to be graphed. A class survey on favorite colors might yield a chart similar to Figure 5–2. Questions such as "Which color has the fewest votes?" or "What do the tally marks for red and blue have in common?" might be asked of students. Students could also be asked to use the tally marks to create a bar graph that shows the same information.

At this level, the data used in pictographs should be sufficient to allow for a scale to be used in representing the information. Remember: always start with a question that gives students a reason for collecting the data in the first place. Consider the following scenario:

> **The cafeteria manager wants to make sure students have an opportunity to buy their dessert at lunch, so she asked Mrs. Gebhart's class to create a survey to find out what food students like best. The survey was given to all twenty-five students in the class. Students were asked to identify their favorite dessert from the following list: pudding, cake, pie, or ice cream.**

$\cancel{||||}$	$\cancel{||||}$ $||$	$||||$
RED	BLUE	GREEN

Figure 5–2 *The results of a class survey on favorite colors*

Narrowing the choices to four possibilities in a survey of twenty-five students provides students with enough meaningful data so they can reach a conclusion about the favorite food of students.

CLASSROOM-TESTED TIP

Creating and administering a survey with a large database would take more time than most teachers want to spend on any one activity, but there are other ways to collect data. For instance, in the cafeteria situation, why not use a number cube, assigning each food to a number? Blank cubes (see Figure 5–3) can also be used, and stickers can be affixed to the sides of the cubes. Students can then write the names of the categories on the stickers and roll the die to collect their data. Working in groups of three to four students, the number of total rolls recorded by the entire class should be equal. Spinners can also be used for this purpose. Clear overhead spinners can be placed on top of predrawn templates with categories written in each of the spaces.

Other topics with possible graphing situations include the following:

■ What is your favorite color?

■ What type of music do you like best?

■ What is your favorite sport to play?

■ What is your favorite sport to watch?

■ What is your favorite flavor of ice cream?

■ What is your favorite food?

■ What kind of pets do you have?

No matter what the topic, remember to begin with a question, and once the data are collected and displayed, use the display to answer the question.

CLASSROOM-TESTED TIP

You can easily create a pictograph by covering one side of an open plain manila folder with a piece of felt. Students could then take their foam shapes or die-cut shapes from a zip-top bag and create instant pictographs in response to any question posed. Even though students may not have an exact representation for the data, as in the food graph, they will get practice in using symbols to represent other types of data and scale.

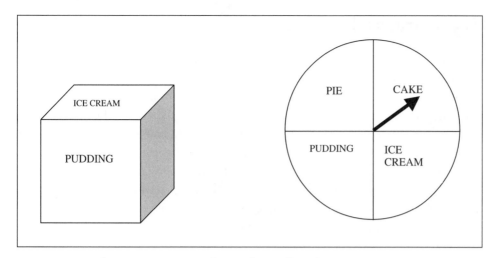

Figure 5–3 *Cubes or spinners can be used to collect data.*

Bar Graphs

For students to understand when to use appropriate data displays, they have to be given multiple opportunities to see how the graphs differ in purpose. Students can use a variety of tools to build bar graphs. Using snap cubes, a student can see how many red cubes there are compared to blue cubes or which color cube has the most in its stack. Showing students that bar graphs can be vertical as well as horizontal provides them with another alternative and allows them to see that their answers don't change just because the position of the graph changes. It is important to have students look at the shape of the data. Sorting objects can also lead to graphing opportunities. Given a set of attribute blocks, pattern blocks, or color tiles, students can sort their shapes or colors and create a graph to represent their manipulatives. Once they have created their graph from their manipulatives, they can take it to the next level and draw their graph on large grid paper.

During many holiday seasons, candy makers market miniature packages with small pieces of candy. These packages can be used to practice estimation skills as well as to create graphs with real-world materials. Each student begins by estimating how many items are in the bag and then counts the items in the bag. Using cards under the graph with the color of the candies written on it, students place their candies above the appropriate spot that corresponds with the color of candy in their bag. Once everyone has placed the candy on the graph, the bar graph begins to takes shape. Keep in mind that the purpose of collecting data is to answer a question, so instead of just graphing for the sake of graphing, the teacher needs to create a legitimate question. The question could center on the number of candies inside or which color was found most often in the bag. Whatever the question, make sure that the data collected are appropriate and provide information that will allow students the opportunity to make an informed conclusion. Students can represent the data on paper as well, coloring in the squares on the grid paper to represent the various pieces of candy.

Try Working Backward

Another way to help students understand continuous graphs is to work backward and start with the graph itself. Then ask students to make up the situation that might have been used to create the graph in the first place.

Students in Mrs. Elwood's first-grade class were given the graph in Figure 5–4 and asked to create a story that would explain what data might have been collected to create this graph. Patty's group wrote that they thought the graph represented the number of different colored birds a bird watcher saw. She saw 5 yellow birds, 5 red birds, and 3 blue birds. Daryl's group took another approach to the situation; they decided that the graph was of different colored cars in the parking lot. There were 5 yellow cars, 5 red cars, and 3 blue cars. Trish's group wrote that they thought it must be a graph of the different colored candies in a package.

Even though the students had not collected the data, each of them was able to describe what might have contributed to that graph display. This type of activity allows students to look closely at the graph and analyze the ups and downs for the type of information that might have been used to create the graph. This activity could also be extended by having students create their own blank graphs for others to analyze or challenging students to draw a graph that might represent a certain situation.

C L A S S R O O M - T E S T E D   T I P

To create a profile of students at the beginning of the year, many teachers take an interest survey to see what sports, TV shows, music, subjects, or foods they like best. Use these surveys to tap into student interests as graphing discussions occur.

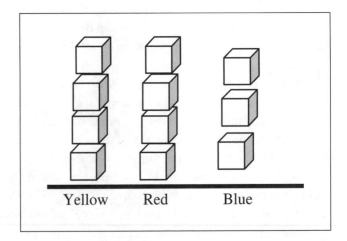

Figure 5–4 *Working backward with a bar graph*

From Concrete to Symbolic

As with other concepts, moving students through the stages of concrete to pictorial to symbolic is crucial in helping them understand graphs. Once students have a clear understanding of what the sections in the graph represent, teachers can move forward in having students create graphs on their own. As their tool kit of graphs grows, they will be able to make decisions about the type of graph that would work best for certain situations. Moving from a real graph to a pictograph can help students understand the purpose of using a key. Assigning a value of two or five to each picture, students can use fewer pictures to represent increasingly larger numbers. Included in this would be the understanding that one-half of a picture represented one-half of the value of one whole picture. It isn't crucial to rush them through this stage; and as this point, keeping the graphs as realistic as possible will students understand the data (Figure 5–5).

The Role of the Teacher

In the area of graphic representations, one of the most important roles a teacher can play is in getting students to see the differences in purpose of certain graphs and how crucial it is to choose the correct representation for the information at hand. Yes, we all know the importance of placing a title on a graph and labeling the *x*- and *y*-axes because that gives important information to the reader, but is it more important than using the appropriate type of graph? Teachers also need to ensure that their students have opportunities to look at data collection and the representation of that data as part of a question to be answered. Using a list of arbitrary numbers does not help students see the importance of graphical display and data analysis. So-called naked math

Figure 5–5 *Sorting objects can lead to graphing opportunities*

serves no purpose in helping students internalize these concepts. Graphing needs to be in context with choices. In the area of data analysis, students can take a lot more meaning away from mean, median, and mode when context is used, but those are not the only analyses of the data and graph that need to take place. In addition to the measures of central tendency, teachers should help students analyze the graph in other ways. By asking questions about the shape of the graphed data or how far apart the data points are, teachers can help students begin to see information about the population being graphed even before they do the computations on the data.

Graphing data is an excellent tool for cross-curricular and multicultural activities. Because textbooks, newspapers, and the Internet are all available as data sources, teachers should make a conscious effort to include multiple opportunities for students to tap into these resources.

Questions for Discussion

1. How can allowing student choice in graphic displays provide information on students' understanding of the purpose of each graph?

2. Why is it important to look at data collection as a means for answering a question?

3. How can teachers help students connect the uses and purposes of the various graphic displays?

4. What are some of the steps that can be used as students are led through the concrete to the symbolic stages of graphing?

5. What are some of the reasons students need context in graphing?

Assessing Students' Representations

Assessment is the process of gathering evidence about a student's knowledge of, ability to use, and disposition toward, mathematics and of making inferences from that evidence for a variety of purposes.

—*Assessment Standards for School Mathematics*,
National Council of Teachers of Mathematics

The ability to represent math ideas in multiple ways is extremely useful as students grow in their mathematical knowledge. By being able to draw on words, pictures, numbers, tables, and so on, students are empowered to understand and represent the world around them and their internal thought processes. However, these models that serve as a student's tool kit must be constructed because they are not taught or given by the teacher. Rather, they emerge from a student's actions in a given situation. When faced with the issue of assessing our students' representations, we must ask ourselves two questions: Why are we assessing the representations our students make, and how are we going to use the information gained from the assessment tool? In this chapter, we discuss the value in assessing those representations, and we look at different ways in which we can assess our students.

Why Assess?

Teachers assess every day, either formally or informally, and for different reasons. The most common assessment we do is that which helps us to make decisions about our instruction. We make daily adjustments to our plans based on our students' needs. Do some students need additional time to explore a topic? Are some students ready to move forward with the application of the concept? Has a group of students already demonstrated mastery of a concept and need to be challenged? Are the majority of students confused about a topic and need a new approach? Assessment is essential in helping us make these decisions.

Another reason we assess is to give parents and students feedback. Most students want to know where they excel and in what areas they need to improve. Parents are especially interested in how their child is performing relative to other students and to the grade-level content. Assessment (especially performance assessment) can help us give them this information. By seeing how their child does when faced with a task with specific objectives, parents can get a clear idea of their child's performance at any given moment. Finally, we may use assessment to help us assign a grade to a student's performance. Evaluating student learning is a complex task that is supported by quality assessment, which can be used to justify a teacher's decision to assign a certain grade to a student.

Assessing Representation

In the primary grades, the main goals of the representation process standard are simply to be able to represent the mathematics and to represent student understanding of the mathematics. Many students will become competent at representing and will look for more accurate and efficient ways to do so; some students will still struggle with what it means to make a representation of their thinking. We all strive to help our students become proficient in mathematics, and all teachers want to be able to judge fairly the work put forth by our students. How, then, do we assess a student's ability to represent his or her thinking? In this book we have been looking at how students can represent their thinking in a number of ways. Words, pictures, diagrams, symbols, and numbers are all elements of what we have been calling multiple representations. But when we assess a student's representations, are we looking for the correctness of the answer? Are we looking for an appropriate algorithm that can be used to solve a problem? Are we evaluating the steps the student went through to reach a solution? Are we assessing only what the student could put down on paper? Are we assessing the conceptual understandings or the procedural ones? And finally, what tools do we use in assessing student representations?

Math classrooms today bear little resemblance to classrooms of ten to fifteen years ago. Gone are the days when students were asked to solve problems without justifying their thinking. Students today are being required to demonstrate their thinking and reasoning through explanations and justifications of their work. We are being challenged to find and use assessments that are rich and have the range of uses that will give our students an opportunity to demonstrate their levels of understanding. If a task is not rich, if it is not cognitively demanding, then students will not be able to adequately demonstrate their knowledge. What information will we gain from a task that has only a right or wrong answer? Today, more than ever, information about students' levels of understanding and mastery is all too important as we look for ways to adjust our instruction to meet the needs not only of our curriculum but more importantly of our students.

We have a number of valuable options available to us when assessing our students' representations (Figure 6–1). We might

■ observe students and engage them in conversations about their work

■ interview and conference with students

■ use a performance-based task

■ collect samples of their work (e.g., portfolios)

The questions are "What should we assess?" and "When should we assess?" Choosing the correct assessment is determined by our purpose in assessing, as described earlier. In this chapter we look at different forms of assessment and determine how we might use them when looking at our students' representations.

Observations

During a math lesson, it is not uncommon for us to walk around and see what our students are doing. Are they on task? Do they appear excited, frustrated, or confused about the activity? Are they working purposefully or merely attempting to appear busy?

Ongoing observations provide teachers with opportunities to see their students in a variety of situations during math class, and while most of those observations are

Figure 6–1 *Students use representations to demonstrate their level of understanding in their work.*

informal in nature, they should be a part of the regular classroom routine. The important thing to remember is that documentation needs to take place during that observation time or shortly thereafter. Without some form of documentation, those mental notes we make as we walk around the room are lost and may fail to provide any lasting information.

One way to make the classroom observation meaningful is to structure a task in which all students are engaged in the same topic at the same time. During the planning of that task, the teacher needs to create a few focused questions to ask during this time and determine how the information will be documented.

Second-grade teacher Mrs. Turner engages in what she likes to call "clipboard cruising." As students are working on an activity, whether cooperatively or independently, she walks around the room with her clipboard, a set of sticky notes, and focus questions. Stopping by Karen's desk, she asks, "How does your representation of the first part of this problem match the question?" If Karen is able to connect her notations to the problem in a meaningful way or if she has created a picture that shows an appropriate level of mastery, Mrs. Turner notes that on Karen's card or sticky note. She may ask one question or a series of questions, but she is always trying to get the students to explain their thinking as they work through the task. Other questions she might ask include "How is your representation of this solution similar to (or different from) one you did yesterday?" "Can you explain the picture you drew for this part of the problem?" and "Why did you choose to organize your work in this way?" As students respond to her questions, she quickly jots down some of their responses on their sticky note. If a student can justify his representation of the problem, if he can provide evidence that he has used his representations to make the problem more meaningful or to find a solution, she makes quick notes of his efforts. She can also clearly see when a student is unable to adequately justify her response or when her representations seem to be taking her in another direction, indicating to the teacher that she needs to find a way to redirect the student's thinking. Once class is over, Mrs. Turner either adds to her notes if time allows or files them in student or class folders for later. Mrs. Turner is looking for a number of things as she cruises the room: is student work organized, have the children been able to communicate their thinking, have they chosen to use one of the problem-solving strategies appropriate for this problem? The observation is purposeful, it is organized, and because Mrs. Turner records the information, it provides lasting evidence of student work. She won't get to all students every day, but it has become a part of her classroom routine, and students know what to expect and aren't surprised or caught off guard when she stops by their desk.

Interviews and Conferences

In addition to observing students as they work, having a structured time to meet with students one on one and confer with them concerning their progress provides valuable information. Planned conferences are a much more structured venue for engaging students in math conversations. Although finding the time to actually have these conversations or interviews with students may be difficult, elementary teachers are wonderfully creative in utilizing stolen moments of time, especially when their efforts yield lasting results.

In Mr. Hampton's first-grade class, he has regularly scheduled interview times with students during recess periods and before or after school when he can focus his attention on a particular student. He starts early in the year talking with his students about the interview process and has an introductory meeting lasting only five to ten minutes when he asks them about their attitudes concerning math. He also likes to see what areas they feel are strengths or weaknesses. Keeping the interview short and nonthreatening is essential to getting students to feel comfortable and willing to talk about their perceived abilities. He tries to make sure he asks each student the same or at least similar questions so that he has like information on each student. As the year progresses, Mr. Hampton continues both formal and informal interviews with his students. Sometimes his inquiries are about a particular task, and he may ask students questions such as, "Why did you choose this representation?" and "Was there another way to solve that problem?" He wants his students to look at alternate methods of solving problems and representing the solutions, so he encourages them to always look back and rethink the problems instead of being satisfied with one method.

In an interview with Robert on his work with the task Bird Legs, Mr. Hampton was particularly interested in how Robert found the answer. He wasn't able to see Robert's thinking, so he asked him how he determined his answer (Figure 6–2). Robert

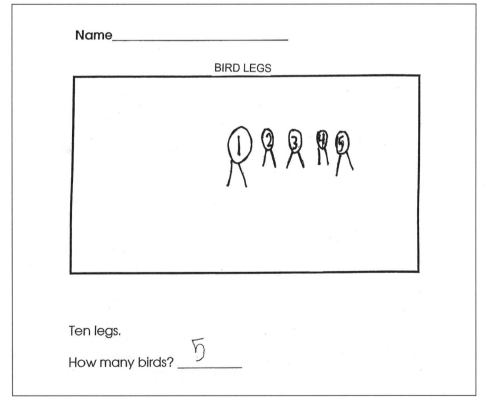

Figure 6–2 *Robert's work on the task Bird Legs*

explained that since he had ten legs and all birds have two legs each, he first drew the legs and then he connected each pair with a circle to represent the birds.

Interviews can be wonderfully enlightening, and taking the time out of a busy schedule to meet one on one with students to discuss their work has huge payoffs in the end.

Performance-Based Tasks

Developing a good performance-based task is sometimes easier said than done. What we think will make a rich question for students to explore sometimes fails to address the mathematics as much as we would like. A performance-based task implies that we want students to do something and that we have identified a product that will serve as proof they have accomplished that task. However, doing an activity for the sake of doing an activity without attention to the mathematics involved is a waste of everyone's time. The first decision a teacher has to make in determining what type of activity to do is what the math is. The second decision must be about the best way to address the concept and whether or not students will be able to demonstrate their knowledge.

Performance tasks are not easy to assess unless the teacher has thought through all of the steps prior to assigning them, and even then adjustments may need to be made once students start working. We sometimes are surprised when we see what students actually read into the problems. An effective task must be relevant to the math, be rich in context, and provide opportunities for students to display their level of thinking. Scoring that task can sometimes be done with a generic rubric or a task-specific checklist. Whatever the criteria, students should be made aware of the criteria prior to starting the task. If the intent of the task is to get at multiple representations of the problem, then that must be a part of the scoring criteria.

Some teachers prefer to score tasks in a holistic fashion. When they create their rubric or scoring checklist, the elements within the tool are applied to the whole product rather than to a single element. For example, in a holistic rubric a teacher might identify three or four elements that can be scored. These elements would all be grouped together, and they would apply to the entire performance, not to individual pieces of that performance. Elements might include items such as completing the task, demonstrating understanding, and showing appropriate representations. The degree to which the student accomplished these elements would determine the score. In an analytic rubric, individual elements, and the degree to which they are each achieved, are scored separately. For example, did the student demonstrate understanding of the problem, and to what degree? Did the student make a plan to solve the problem, and to what degree?

Whether holistic or analytic, the rubric needs to have as one of its elements descriptions of how the representations will be scored. An element on a rubric associated with representations might read: "Communicates thinking clearly, using appropriate words, computation, diagrams, charts, or other representations." If students know ahead of time that the representation element is equally as important as the answer, they can attend to that portion of their response. Rubrics used in scoring tasks need to be easy to apply, and the score should not be difficult to determine. The more opportunities students have to be assessed using a rubric, the more comfortable they'll become with the process. If a task-specific scoring tool is needed, you can create a checklist that resembles the rubric but that has specific information about that one assignment.

C L A S S R O O M - T E S T E D   T I P

Pinch Card Scoring

Write the numbers 0, 1, 2, and 3 down the side of index cards. As you walk around the room and observe students at work either independently or in small groups, you can pinch a card next to the score you would give their work at that point and hand the card to the student or group. This way no other students become aware of the score and the student can get quick feedback on her efforts and adjust as necessary. You can also make cards for students so that they can self-score their efforts.

Portfolios—Collections of Student Work

Portfolios allow students an opportunity to showcase their work. They also provide teachers and parents with a picture album that summarizes a student's progress and efforts. Assessments should not be snapshots in time; rather, they should capture a student at various places along the learning continuum. By carefully structuring the collection of student work, a teacher can gather evidence of growth and information on how a student's mathematical thinking has developed. Portfolios of student work need to be structured from the start. It isn't enough to just ask students to put evidence of their work in a folder. Instead, we need to be clear about the type of work we are expecting students to submit. For that reason, it is important to list for students some of the criteria they need to consider as they select work samples. In the area of representations, we want students to select work that shows both their thinking and their ability to use multiple representations. They need to include samples of work that show that they

- used pictures to help them reach a solution

- used graphic representations of the data (more than one sample)

- used words to explain how they developed their solution

- used words to justify why their solution was correct

- used a graphic organizer to illustrate a procedure

- used more than one representation to reach their solution

- worked with a group to solve a problem

If the criteria for assessing the portfolio collection are made clear to students beforehand and they have a checklist of desired elements, they can begin assembling their work at the start of the school year. As they find better examples of a certain type of work, they can replace previous selections.

In Mrs. Malone's second-grade class, her students regularly update and add to their portfolio collections. She hands each one of them a criteria checklist at the beginning of the year and goes over how they are to select work samples for their portfolios. She also lists some required pieces, such as formative assessment samples and journal entries on certain topics. The students are ultimately responsible for the rest of the collection. At the end of the year, she has her students go through their portfolios one more time and review all of the pieces they have chosen. At that time she asks each student to select one piece of work that the child is most proud of creating, and she invites parents in for an afternoon of sharing portfolio samples. Parents first walk around the room, looking at the various pieces of student work, and then she has the students present their one sample that they chose from all of their work pieces. The students explain why this is a good work sample and what they have learned from the assignment, and then they show how the sample meets the criteria. This activity creates wonderful communication between students, the teacher, and parents, and at the same time it provides additional motivation for students in making careful selections along the way because they know their parents will be in to look through all of the samples. At the end of the gallery walk, Mrs. Malone encourages parents to take their child's collection of work samples and share it with next year's teacher at an appropriate time.

Assessment Equity

With the growing trend toward full inclusion, teachers today have more challenges than ever in making sure students are assessed fairly and equitably. All students must be assessed, but how do you assess students with special needs and report their performance with clarity? In assessing representations, the answer may be a little easier than in other areas because alternative representations do, in fact, have a tendency to meet the needs of our special learners. Here are some suggestions:

- *Provide a Frame or Context for the Problem:* Many of our lesson plans and assessment documents can be adapted so students can answer in an alternate form. For example, instead of asking a student to answer a question such as "Which is greater, one-half or one-fourth?" you can ask the student to place the two fractions on a number line. By asking the question in this manner and providing the number line or a ruler, you present the student with a framework for the question, which may allow the student to more easily determine which fraction is larger when considering their placement on a number line. You might also ask the student to represent the two fractions in a drawing, which would give you even more information about the child's understanding of the relative size of the two fractions.

■ *Use Manipulatives:* Continue the availability of manipulatives during assessments. By making classroom tools available during assessment time, you help all students feel comfortable accessing them as they work through problems. The students can work the solutions out using the manipulatives and then make the appropriate representations on paper.

■ *Conduct Group Assessments:* Consider allowing students to take an assessment as a group. In this type of assessment, students will feel free to discuss the mathematics and also will show each other how they would represent their ideas either pictorially or numerically.

■ *Make Use of Technology:* There are a number of opportunities today to have students demonstrate their knowledge using technology. Teachers can use virtual manipulatives to help students solve problems and then have them translate the pictures to their own work. Interactive white board technology has brought a wonderful new engaging element to all classrooms. Students and teachers can manipulate base ten blocks right on the wall or change the shape of polygons by dragging the pen across the board. Students in the primary grades can also make use of handheld technology. This small but powerful tool can help students see alternate representations as well as create their own drawings and beam the completed solution to their teacher who could then display the final solution on the board.

Feedback

The purpose of assessment is to provide information, and that information needs to be used to inform instruction. What do we do with the evidence we collect on our students' performance? We can begin by asking questions about some of the student work we collect. Have the students communicated their solutions with appropriate words, numbers, and pictures? What mathematical thinking is evidenced in their work? What are some of the differences in the ways students found results? We also need to be mindful of the task we have given them and ask ourselves if it provided us with the information we thought it would or if we need to revise the task to make it richer. Do we have sufficient information on how the students have performed as compared with the standards, and if not, what do we need to do to help them improve?

Finally, what information can we provide parents about their children? Assessment is no longer about a grade, it is no longer about a moment in time, and it is no longer about just an answer without an explanation of process or justification for procedure. Assessment needs to be ongoing, informative, and accessible to all students. Having students skilled in solving problems using a variety of representation strategies is a goal that we all can set for ourselves and for our students. If we are to help our students grow in the math competencies, we need to provide them with as many strategies as possible along the way. We need to continue to look for and create assessment items that give our students multiple pathways to achieving success.

Questions for Discussion

1. What are some of the ways students can be assessed?

2. How can student interviews provide insight into our students' thinking?

3. What advantages can be found in using rubrics for scoring tools?

4. What feedback can we supply students about their assessment data?

5. How can the use of representations help in our assessment of special needs students?

7

Representation Across the Content Standards

Students in the elementary and middle grades use a variety of forms of representation to record and communicate their thinking: symbols, drawings and pictures, tables and charts, physical materials, graphs, models, and oral and written language.

—Suzanne Chapin, Catherine O'Connor, and Nancy Anderson,
Classroom Discussions: Using Math Talk to Help Students Learn

We have been focusing on helping our students develop the ability to represent their thinking and the mathematical concepts they are learning about. Being able to represent thinking both externally and internally will enable students to approach novel situations with many strategies from which to choose. Symbols, drawings and pictures, tables and charts, graphs, manipulatives, models, and oral and written language are just some of these representations. Representation, however, is only one of five different process standards set forth by the National Council of Teachers of Mathematics (2000). The other four include problem solving, reasoning and proof, communication, and connections. Representation is interconnected to each of these other processes. When problem solving, students might use representations in the form of pictures to help them understand the problem, and then they might represent their solution in the form of an equation. They use reasoning skills to infer and decipher information, and they might use representations to justify their answer to a problem. To communicate their thought processes, students might create a representation in the form of a diagram or an equation. Students connect math concepts to other math concepts and to the world around them, and representations such as a graph or manipulatives can help to show these connections.

Just as the process standards are interconnected, we must connect content to those process standards in a meaningful way. NCTM (2000) has outlined content standards in five areas: number and operations, algebra, geometry, measurement, and data analysis and probability. In this chapter, we look at how the use of representations can be developed and used across the content standards. In each section, we give an overview of a lesson or problem task related to the content standard, highlight the use of representation in the lesson or activity, and discuss the mathematics involved.

Number and Operations

Students who understand the structure of numbers and the relationships among numbers can work with them flexibly. (NCTM 2000, 149)

The same type of thinking can be assessed when looking at problems with multiple solutions.

The Problem Task

Mrs. Gebhart presented the following problem to her second-grade class:

I have seven bones and two dogs. I want to give an even number of bones to one dog. I want to give an odd number of bones to the other dog.

Students were given a small bag of candy bones to work with as their manipulatives and a page to record all of their responses. Any manipulative would work for this problem; cereal, beans, two-color counters, or snap cubes could all be used by students. The important point is to give them a tool that helps them visualize the distribution of the bones to odd or even. She did not tell them at first about the number of possible solutions; instead, she challenged them to find one solution. At first the students were not quite sure how to record their answers or set up the solution area, so they discussed what needed to be recorded. Together, rereading the problem, they decided they needed two dogs and that one dog would be labeled O for odd and the other dog would be labeled E for even. Once they drew their dogs and labeled them, they distributed the manipulative bones to each dog. The question was raised as to whether or not the odd dog could get all seven bones, which meant the even dog would have zero. They decided that zero fit the solution even though most of them thought it wasn't fair that one dog got all of the bones, and how could you give a dog zero bones? The manipulatives were used to find a solution, and the students recorded that representation on their paper. As they worked toward finding their solution, they also provided the number sentence to support their picture. The students then shared their answer with their neighbors, and it was at this point that a few of them began to realize that this problem must have more than one solution. Rather than provide the answers, Mrs. Gebhart challenged her students to find as many answers as they could. Most of the students were able to find at least two different solutions. Georgia was able to find four different solutions and organize all four of her answers (Figure 7–1). She also used pictorial representations along with the appropriate numeric support. Her four solutions show not only her ability to find multiple solutions but her ability to present those answers in an organized format.

About the Math

Problem-solving experiences with manipulatives give students opportunities to clarify concepts and skills that are all too often forgotten when students fail to internalize the processes. Even though this problem was challenging for some students, in that multiple solutions were possible, the numbers were manageable and the context was fun so the students were motivated to find as many answers as possible (Figure 7–2). Mrs. Gebhart could very easily have told them from the start how many solutions were possible, but this would turn the focus of the activity away from thinking about the problem to just finding X number of solutions. Several other elements need to be considered in doing a problem-solving activity with young students. The most important of those elements is the fine line teachers walk in letting students construct

Figure 7–1 *Georgia's amazing four solutions to the Dog Bones problem*

Figure 7–2 *Georgia is hard at work solving the Dog Bones problem.*

meaning out of the math and weighing that independence against the level of frustration they experience. "The fact that representations are such effective tools may obscure how difficult it was to develop them and more important, how much work it takes to understand them" (NCTM 2000). With young learners who do not have an extensive tool kit of strategies, teacher guidance and modeling is necessary to reach a successful conclusion.

CLASSROOM-TESTED TIP

Purchase packages of inexpensive plastics cups in red, yellow, and green. When students are engaged in small-group work, give them a stack of three plastic cups, one of each color. As the students are working, they should have their green cup at the top of their stack. If they begin to experience problems along the way, they need to put the yellow cup on top. The yellow cup tells you that the students are having a little trouble but they are still working. With the yellow cup on top, students know to try to figure out how to continue without the teacher's help. The last resort is the red cup. When the red cup goes on top, it is a signal for the teacher that the group can't continue without assistance and they need help *now*. If cups aren't available, use laminated signs in red, yellow, and green that students can put on the corner of their desk. The cups reassure the students that they can ask for help but that they need to try to work things out first. The teacher is always the last resort.

Algebra

More and more teachers are being asked to foster algebraic thinking at all grade levels. Today, the big ideas of algebra—equivalence, properties, and variables—show up in all primary classrooms. When students think of algebra, they think of variables, and the very abstract nature of the standard makes teaching it all that much harder. For students to understand the generalized nature of algebra, they need to see the connections to arithmetic at each grade level. For this reason, problems that provide students with opportunities to make those connections need to begin early.

The Problem Task

The following activity, conducted with a group of twenty kindergartners, explores repeating patterns. Much of the experience with patterns for these young students to this point had centered around their morning calendar routine. Each date piece on the calendar was represented by a shape, which, after several days, formed an identifiable repeating pattern, such as circle, square, circle, square, and so on.

The teacher, Mrs. Emilie, gathered the students in a circle and asked what they knew about patterns. The children were eager to share their responses, and several hands went up. Mrs. Emilie called on a few children to share.

MICHAELA: Patterns are like red, blue, red, blue.

ALONZO: Sometimes a pattern goes boy, girl, boy, girl, boy, girl.

MIN: I see a pattern in the blinds on the window: light, dark, light, dark, light, dark, light, dark.

TEACHER: I can see that you have been thinking about patterns and where you see them. Now I am going to make a listening pattern with my hands, and when you think you have figured out the pattern, you can join in.

Mrs. Emilie clapped her hands, then patted her knees, and repeated this sequence several times. After about five seconds of observing her perform this pattern, students started to join in, clapping their hands, then patting their knees, and then repeating. Mrs. Emilie asked if anyone could tell about this pattern in words.

Krystal raised her hand and said, "It goes clap-pat-clap-pat and keeps going."

"Great!" responded Mrs. Emilie. "Does anyone think they can describe the pattern with ABCs?" No one offered a response, so Mrs. Emilie said, "We can describe a clap-pat-clap-pat- pattern with the letters, A-B-A-B and so on. Now I'm going to start a new pattern.

The new pattern involved clapping twice and then patting knees. After just a few seconds, several students joined in and copied the pattern. After waiting for most students to join in, Mrs. Emilie asked, "Who can describe, or tell about, this pattern in words?"

Christopher shouted out excitedly, "Clap-clap-pat-clap-clap-pat!" Soon all the children were saying the pattern as they performed it.

Mrs. Emilie then asked, "Can anyone describe this pattern using ABCs?"

Jonas responded, "A-A-B-A-A-B."

"OK, let's say those letters as we do the pattern. A-A-B-A-A-B . . ." Mrs. Emilie said. It was clear that some of the students had difficulty following the pattern and assigning a representation to it, such as letters or words. Mrs. Emilie made a mental note of those students who were struggling with the concept.

Mrs. Emilie modeled a few more listening patterns, and then asked for volunteers to lead the group in a pattern. The children enthusiastically followed their classmate's patterns, and some shouted out the words and letters that matched the pattern.

The next part of the lesson involved manipulatives. Mrs. Emilie pulled out a tub of one-inch square tiles and asked the students to watch as she created a pattern with them. Using two colors, she created an A-B-A-B pattern. When she had repeated the pattern several times, she asked someone to describe her pattern.

Tatiana responded, "It goes yellow-green-yellow-green-yellow-green, and keeps going."

"OK," Mrs. Emilie said. "Who thinks they can use letters to describe this pattern?"

Lee raised his hand. "It goes A-B-A-B-A-B-A-B."

"Great! Now, I'm going to change my pattern a little bit." Mrs. Emilie spread her pattern out and slipped a red tile in after each yellow tile. She ended on a yellow tile. "Who thinks they can tell about this pattern now?"

Andrew shouted out, "Now it's yellow-red-green-yellow-red-green-yellow. The next tile will be red!"

"How do you know?" asked Mrs. Emilie.

"Because it goes yellow-red-green-yellow-red-green-yellow-RED. It starts over and over so red would come next," answered Andrew proudly.

"How could we describe this pattern with ABCs?" she then asked.

"It goes A-B-C-A-B-C-A and B would come next," responded Jennifer.

"How do you know?" questioned Mrs. Emilie.

"Because the red is B and the red comes next, and the yellow is A and the green is C."

The students were then invited to use the tiles to create their own patterns, and several students were asked to share the pattern they made, describing it in as many ways as they could.

The final activity required students to return to their tables and create another pattern with the tiles. They were then to make a paper representation of their pattern using one-inch squares of various colors, which they would glue down. In Figure 7–3 we see two different students' work. The first sample shows an A-B-A-B pattern. Not all students were able to assign letters to their patterns, but this student seemed to understand the concept. The second sample in Figure 7–3 shows a pattern made by a student who is starting to get the idea of a repeating pattern, but she included an extra tile in the middle. She did not attempt to assign letters to each component of the pattern.

About the Math

This activity was rich because it included several different content and process standards. Students were challenged to communicate about their patterns and to justify their reasoning about why their creation represented a pattern, as well as how they

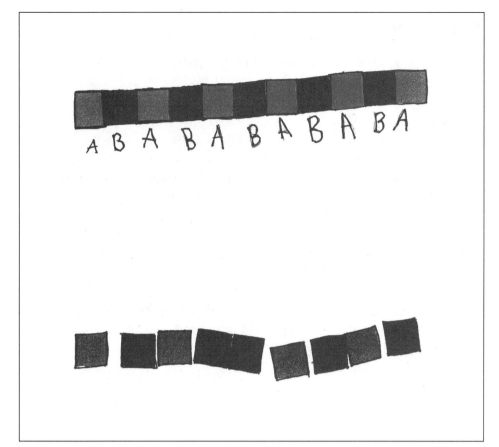

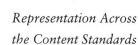

Figure 7–3 *Two students' efforts to represent the A-B-A-B pattern*

knew what would come next in the pattern. They demonstrated beginning algebraic reasoning when they allowed a symbol (in this case a letter) to represent the structure of the pattern, such as A-B-C-A-B-C for red-yellow-blue-red-yellow-blue, understanding that the A stood for red, the B for yellow, and the C for blue. Finally, they were able to practice their developing knowledge of patterns by creating concrete and paper representations of them. As mentioned throughout this book, "The very act of generating a concrete representation establishes an image of the knowledge in students' minds" (Marzano et al. 2001, 78). The range of sophistication in the different patterns that the students created gave Mrs. Emilie some useful information to guide her instruction in patterning. Sample follow-up activities to this lesson might include centers with collections of different materials, such as seashells, bread tags, pebbles, small plastic bugs, and so on, to provide opportunities for students to practice and further develop their understanding of repeating patterns. She might also make some pattern cards on tag board that students could copy and extend with concrete materials. In addition, rubber stamps provide students with a fun material to use to create repeating patterns.

Geometry

Geometry is a significant branch of mathematics, the one most visible in the physical world. (Burns 2002, 79)

Children have a natural curiosity about geometry. From an early age, they manipulate shapes, observing how they are similar and different, seeing how they fit together, and using them to create designs. They enjoy pointing out familiar shapes in their environment and experimenting with combining shapes to create new shapes. It is our role to help develop students' spatial abilities, and we should use varied experiences to help students connect geometry to ideas in number, patterns, and measurement. Students in prekindergarten through grade 2 are learning to describe and identify shapes by name. They also are manipulating shapes, exploring the concepts of motion, location, and orientation. "Students should use their notions of geometric ideas to become more proficient in describing, representing, and navigating their environment" (NCTM 2000, 97). By embedding these experiences in problem-solving activities, we encourage students to investigate patterns in shapes and to use reasoning skills in a spatial context.

The Lesson

This lesson was conducted in a second-grade class. The teacher, Mr. Hanna, used the concept formation model to introduce the concept of symmetry, and students were then given an independent task to explore the concept (see Representation Across the Content Standards section of the CD).

After gathering the students at the front of the room, Mr. Hanna showed an example and a nonexample of symmetry using multicolor one-inch tiles on the overhead. He asked the students to simply look at the two designs and think about how they might be similar or different. He then created another example and nonexample (Figure 7–4) and asked the students to first think by themselves about what they noticed, and then they were asked to turn to their learning partner and share their thoughts. One pair of students focused on the number of tiles: six in the examples and four in the nonexamples. Another pair noticed that the examples and nonexamples had some of the same colors, but that they were in different places. Mr. Hanna then put the last set of examples and nonexamples up. There were some "Oohs" as the children noticed that now the example had four tiles and the nonexample had six tiles. He let the students look at the six figures for a minute silently and then directed them again to discuss with their partner.

Some of the students were confused by the change in the number of tiles, and they had difficulty moving beyond this property. Others, however, began to notice properties of symmetry. Comments such as these could be heard:

"The colors are in the same place in the examples."
"In the nonexamples, the colors aren't in any order."

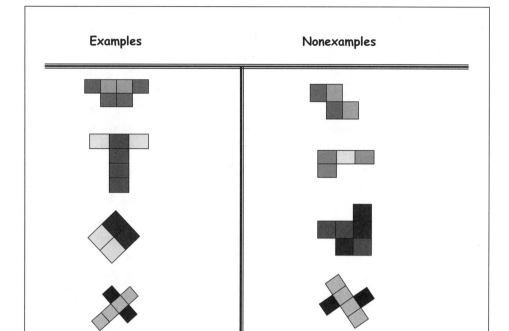

Figure 7–4 *Concept formation for symmetry*

"In the examples, the tiles are in a design. In the nonexamples, the tiles are just
    put together any old way."

Although their language is not precise at this point, the children are making some
observations about symmetry. Mr. Hanna refocused the students and asked them
what they noticed about the colors of the tiles.

Tatiana raised her hand and said, "I noticed that the colors were in the same
places in each side of the design."

Sammy said, "Yeah, like if there's a blue on this side, there's one on the other
side. In the nonexamples, the colors don't match on each side."

"So you're saying the colors have to match on each side of the design?" asked
Mr. Hanna. Most of the kids nodded their heads, and Sammy replied, "Yes."

"OK. Now let's look at how the tiles are put together. What do you notice?"
continued Mr. Hanna.

Alex said, "In the nonexamples, they don't make a neat design. In the examples,
the tiles are in order."

Mr. Hanna probed further, "What do you mean by order?"

"Well," Alex continued, "each side matches. It's like you can draw a line in the
middle and the sides match, but in the nonexamples you can't do that."

Mr. Hanna put one more example and nonexample up. The children excitedly
began talking to each other about what they saw.

"The colors are the same," noted one student.

"Yeah, but they're in different places," said her learning partner.

"In the example, it's like you could fold it in half and the sides would match up. In the nonexample, you can't do that because the black tiles are in different places," observed another student.

"Do we all agree that in the examples you can draw a line somewhere on the figure and the parts of the figure on each side of the line will match?" Mr. Hanna asked them. The children nod their heads. "And on the nonexamples, we can't draw a line and have the sides match, right?" Again, they nod their heads. Mr. Hanna then calls up different students to "prove" the conjectures the children have made using an uncooked spaghetti noodle.

Matt uses the spaghetti noodle to show that in the first example he can lay it vertically to split the figure in two halves, each matching the other. He tries to do the same with the nonexample, laying the noodle both vertically and then horizontally, but demonstrates that it cannot be done. Mariella then comes up to the overhead to "prove" that the remaining examples can be divided using the spaghetti noodle to show "mirrored" images, whereas the nonexamples cannot.

"What we have been looking at are examples and nonexamples of symmetry. Let me show you how you can use a mirror to test for symmetry," says Mr. Hanna.

He gathers the children on one side of the overhead and takes a small, rectangular mirror and places it vertically in the first example. He asks the children to look in the mirror. He then lifts the mirror and asks the children what they see. They noticed that the image they saw in the mirror is exactly the same as the image they see when the mirror is lifted. Mr. Hanna continues to do the same with the other examples, and the kids are excited to see that each time the images are the same. He then uses the mirror on the nonexamples, rotating it in different ways. Each time he lifts the mirror, the kids shout out, "It's not the same!"

"Who thinks they can explain what symmetry means?" asks Mr. Hanna.

Mr. Hanna writes up the different responses the children offer, and then asks someone to come up with one sentence that describes symmetry. The definition they agree on is this:

Symmetry is when you can draw a line on a design or shape and one side matches the other side exactly.

Although the children are describing only *line symmetry,* as opposed to rotational symmetry, Mr. Hanna does not make the distinction between the two. That concept will be introduced later.

He then directs the students to put their hands together and then open them "like a book." The children notice that their hands match up almost perfectly with each other when closed and that, when open, you can draw a line between the two matching sides. After allowing the students a few minutes to find more examples of symmetry on their bodies and around the room, he is ready to continue with the next part of the lesson.

Mr. Hanna asks the children to use one-inch colorful tiles to create their own symmetrical design. After creating their design, they are to transfer it to a paper representation using one-inch grid paper and crayons. As seen in Figure 7–5, one student

Figure 7–5 *One student's representation of symmetry*

created a design onto which he drew a black line, indicating the line of symmetry. As the children worked at their tables, it was clear who understood the concept of symmetry and who had some confusion. Mr. Hanna was able to pull a few students over to a side table to further develop the concept with them while the rest of the class worked independently.

About the Math

In this lesson students were asked to make observations and conclusions about the mathematical concept of symmetry, and they formulated their own definition of the concept. They made conjectures, which they then had to prove or disprove, which helped to solidify the concept in their minds. Using tiles to create their own examples of symmetry, students drew on their spatial reasoning skills and helped to form an image in their minds of what symmetry means and might look like. Finally, transferring their design or figure to one-inch grid paper helped them to make the link between three-dimensional representations and two-dimensional ones.

Sample follow-up activities to the lesson might include centers where the children are given different materials such as pattern blocks, toothpicks, multilink cubes, uncooked spaghetti noodles, and mirrors and asked to create examples of symmetry and record their representations on paper. Alternatively, they may be asked to find all the examples of symmetry that they can in the classroom, school, playground, nature, and so forth.

Measurement

> Measurement is a process that students in grades 3–5 use every day as they explore questions related to their school or home environment. (NCTM 2000, 171)

Measurement, like geometry, is an area in which children have a natural curiosity. Even very young children enjoy using tools such as rulers and measuring tapes to measure the length of objects, and they experiment with different concepts in measurement, such as time: "I'm coming to your house at fourteen o'clock!" In the primary grades, students are beginning to gain an understanding that objects have attributes, and it is those attributes that we measure, such as length, height, weight, and so on. Their concept of time is becoming more realistic, and they can begin to apply their knowledge of time to different situations, such as how much time remains before lunch or how long it takes to get to Grandma's house. They also begin to have more of an appreciation for units of volume and begin to develop benchmarks in their minds, such as a gallon jug, a two-liter soda bottle, and a pint of milk. It is important for teachers to help students connect ideas within measurement with other mathematical concepts and other disciplines, such as art and music.

In prekindergarten through grade 2, students are learning what it means to measure an object. Through many varied and hands-on activities, students begin to deepen their understanding that we first must identify an attribute to be measured, and then choose an appropriate unit and tool with which to measure. In the following task, students were asked to investigate the attribute of length using various materials.

The Problem Task

Before posing this task to her first-grade students, Mrs. Hall asked students what they knew about measurement. "What does it mean to measure something?" she asked.

Responses included, "It's how tall you are," or "You can measure how much water a cup holds." It was obvious that this group of students had had some experiences with measuring and could associate the concept with familiar objects and ideas. Mrs. Hall explained to the children that they were going to do a measurement investigation and posed the following task:

Trace your hand in the space below. Choose a unit to measure the length of your hand. Estimate how many units long your hand is. Then measure your hand with the units.

Before asking the students to complete the task independently, Mrs. Hall modeled the activity. First, she asked students to look at one of their hands and decide which part of their hand they would measure if they were to going to investigate how long it was. William responded, "You measure the middle finger." Mrs. Hall asked him to explain. "Well, the middle finger is the longest one, so that is what you measure," he replied. She pushed further. "William says that we should measure the middle finger. How can we use our middle finger to find out how long our whole hand is?"

Brandon answered, "We can measure from the bottom of our hand here (*pointing to the base of the hand at the wrist*) to the top of our middle finger."

"Why is it important to measure to the top of our middle finger rather than, say, to the top of our pinky or our pointer finger?" Mrs. Hall asked.

Cindy raised her hand. "Because if we measure to the top of our pinky, that's shorter, and we won't find out how long our whole hand is."

Mrs. Hall noticed many children nodding their heads in agreement. "So, can we say that to measure the length of our hand, we must measure from the bottom of our hand to the top of our middle finger?" The children nod and say yes.

Mrs. Hall modeled on the overhead projector how the children would trace around their hand. She then showed them the units from which they could choose: foam fish cutouts, centimeter cubes, one-inch tiles, and one-inch plastic sticks. Choosing the fish as the first unit she would use, Mrs. Hall asked the children how she should use the fish to measure the length of her hand. Jae-Hoon suggested putting the fish in a straight line from the bottom of her traced hand to the top of her middle finger. "Why is it important to line up the fish in a straight line?" she asked.

Jae-Hoon responded, "You have to put them in a straight line or else they will go all over and you won't know how long your hand is."

Mrs. Hall then asked, "If I wanted to use the fish with the tiles to measure how long my hand is, is that OK?"

Some children nodded their heads, but Claudia said, "No, you can't use different things together. Everything has to be the same size."

Mrs. Hall asked the class, "What is Claudia saying?"

Ryan responded, "She's saying that you have to measure with things that are the same size, because if you use different things, like a fish and a tile, you wouldn't know what to call it."

Although their explanations were not entirely complete, the children were showing some real developing understandings of fundamental concepts related to measuring the attribute of length: that the units being used to measure must be of uniform size.

"OK," said Mrs. Hall, "so before we measure the length of my hand, let's estimate how many fish long my hand is."

Estimates ranged from three to twenty. Mrs. Hall accepted all estimates without commenting on any, helping the children to see that when estimating, there is no right or wrong answer. She then took the fish and laid them one at a time on the length of her hand, from the bottom to the tip of her middle finger. "Five!" the children said excitedly when she was done. "So," she continued, "who estimated a number near five?" Sebastian raised his hand. "Friends, I want you to listen carefully to what Sebastian says now so that you can explain what he did. Sebastian, what number did you estimate and why?"

Sebastian answered, "I estimated six because I was thinking about how big each fish was, and I was trying to see it in my head if you put the fish in a line on your hand."

"Can someone else explain what Sebastian was thinking when he estimated six fish?" Mrs. Hall asked the other students.

Sara raised her hand. "He said that he looked at how big each fish was, and he was thinking in his head how the fish would look when you put them in a line on your hand."

Mrs. Hall used a strategy to highlight one student's approach to estimating. She asked the student to tell how he did it, and then asked another student to repeat back what she heard. This helps the students cue in when another student is speaking, and it ensures that the whole group hears a particularly successful strategy more than one time. If no one had been able to paraphrase what Sebastian had said, Mrs. Hall would have asked him to explain it again to the group.

After asking someone to repeat back what the students were to do when they got back to their seats, Mrs. Hall sent them back to their tables. The students found a recording sheet for each of them and containers of fish, cubes, tiles, and plastic sticks on their tables.

As they got to work, Mrs. Hall reminded her students to estimate the number of units needed first, and then measure using the units (see Figure 7–6). Many students used the information they had learned from the lesson introduction and estimated that their hands would also be five fish long. However, they discovered that, for the most part, their hands were four fish long.

"Why do you think your hand was four fish long while mine was five fish long?" Mrs. Hall asked Timothy.

"I think it's because your hand is bigger than mine because you're bigger than I am," he replied.

Mrs. Hall continued to circulate, asking questions to promote thinking and clarifying the task when necessary. She saw that Jose had written down four as his estimate for the number of centimeter cubes needed. She asked him why he estimated four, and he said he didn't know. She asked him to compare the size of the centimeter cube with the fish, which he had already used. He said that the cube was smaller than the fish.

"I see that your hand was four fish long," Mrs. Hall said. "If the cube is smaller than the fish, do you think you will need more cubes or fewer cubes to measure the length of your hand?"

Name_____ Date_____

Trace your hand in the space below. **Choose a unit** to measure the length of your hand. **Estimate** how many units long your hand is. Then **measure** your hand with the units.

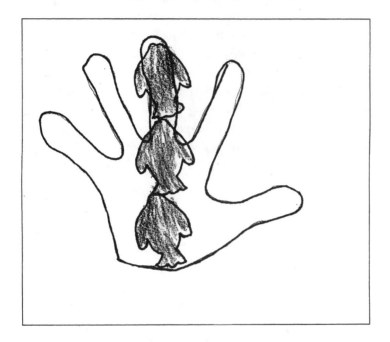

Units I Used	Estimate	Actual
Fish	5	3
tile	4	4
CuBe	9	11

Figure 7–6 *A student measures her hand with nonstandard units*

"I think maybe more," he replied.

"Why do you think you will need more cubes than fish?" she continued.

"I think because since they're smaller, it will take more to make a line from here to here (*pointing to bottom of hand and tip of middle finger*)."

"Try it and see what you discover. I'll come back." Returning after a few minutes, Mrs. Hall noticed that Jose had written down ten cubes as his estimate and had lined up thirteen cubes along the length of his hand.

"What did you discover, Jose?" prompted Mrs. Hall.

"I discovered that my hand is thirteen cubes long, which is a lot more than four."

Without this investigative questioning, Mrs. Hall might not have been able to uncover the misunderstandings in Jose's mind and help him to create meaning on his own about the concept of unit size and how it relates to measurement.

Students who finished the task quickly were invited to take one of the one-inch plastic sticks and search around their classroom for items that were the same length. When it was clear most students had finished the activity, she asked them to regroup on the carpet. "What did you discover in this investigation?" she asked the class.

"I discovered that my hand is four fish long," replied Cecelia.

"I discovered that my hand is five tiles long and five sticks long," said Allen.

"Did anyone else discover that it took the same number of tiles as it did sticks to measure their hand?" asked Mrs. Hall. Several students raised their hands. "Why do you think that happened?" she asked.

Christina responded, "I think they must have been the same size, that's why they both were five." The discussion continued for a few more minutes, with students sharing discoveries they made and Mrs. Hall helping them to make connections.

About the Math

Students were actively engaged in this interesting and motivating activity. Using an investigation model, a question was posed (How long is your hand?), and students were invited to use appealing manipulatives to complete the task. The attribute of length was investigated in a concrete way, and by experimenting with nonstandard units of different sizes, students were given the opportunity to develop their own understandings about the concept. Probing questions encouraged the students to think more deeply about the math, and the discussion after the task enabled students to further make connections and process the learning that they had done.

Data Analysis: Statistics and Probability

Learning to interpret, use, and construct useful representations needs careful and deliberate attention in the classroom. (NCTM 2000, 207)

The purpose of data analysis is to answer an engaging question, a question that has real implications and that can be answered by collecting, organizing, displaying, and interpreting data. Students in prekindergarten through grade 2 should have multiple opportunities to interpret data and decide which data display to use. Only by using a variety of data displays that are both real and meaningful will students understand the factors involved in making those decisions. Because the very act of collecting data is the direct result of asking a question, that question occasionally leads to a prediction about the data results, which can take place prior to the data being collected but also after the data have been collected and analyzed. Before collecting data, the teacher might ask, "What do you think the data will show?" Or once the data have been collected, he could ask, "What do you think will happen next?" It is because of this close relationship that the terms *statistics* and *probability* are usually encompassed in the term *data analysis*.

Simulations involving probability have not always been prevalent in prekindergarten through grade 2, and for that reason, little has been done in this area beyond activities dealing with what sums are more likely to come up when rolling two dice or flipping a coin one hundred times and seeing if you get an equal number of heads and tails. Issues dealing with probability are all around us, and more and more curricula are elevating the importance of this topic within the data analysis strand. No longer is the topic of probability relegated to the end of the curriculum, where it may or may not be covered. Probability simulations are among the most meaningful activities for students, and they are relatively easy to plan and fun to implement.

The Problem Task

The following activity was conducted in Mr. Cuppett's second-grade classroom as part of his unit on probability. Students were working on the idea of fairness as it relates to games of chance. Fairness in games is a pretty familiar topic for students, so it doesn't take much to get them engaged in the activity. Before starting the activity, Mr. Cuppett asked students to think about the topic of fairness and how that plays into games of chance. Several of the students talked about games they had played at carnivals and about their parents playing the lottery and how they thought some games couldn't be won. Steven said he had played a dart game at the fair and lost every time. Mr. Cuppett asked him if that was because of the way the game was set up or because of his dart-throwing skills! He gave each of the students in his class two number cubes, a two-color counter, and a sheet with the numbers 1–12 in the boxes (Figure 7–7).

The students were told to roll their cubes and record the two numbers on their paper and find the sum. Every time they found a sum, they were to mark an X in the column above that number. For example: if a student rolled a 3 and 4, the sum would be 7 and an X would be placed above the 7. Sarah raised her hand to ask about the two-color counter she was given. Mr. Cuppett replied that he wanted them to place

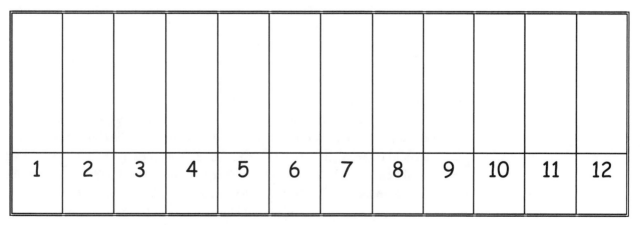

Figure 7–7 *Recording sheet for probability study*

that counter on the chart before they started on the number they thought would have the most Xs above it at the end of the game. Charlie immediately decided to place his counter on 12 because he was sure he could roll doubles many times. Sarah decided to place her counter on the 3. When questioned about why she chose 3, Sarah couldn't explain her reason; she just liked the number. Every person in the group was to roll their dice a total of twenty times and find the sum each time. The students all began rolling their dice, adding their numbers and marking their papers. Charlie decided early on that perhaps he hadn't made such a wise decision since he hadn't rolled a single double sixes and he only had four rolls remaining. Sarah was faring a little better, as she had two Xs in the column above her chosen number. As the students completed this first round, most of them discovered two things: (1) they were getting better and quicker at adding the two dice together, and (2) they should have made a different guess as to which number they thought would be found most often.

Rather than engage the class in a discussion at this point, Mr. Cuppett told the students to use another chart to repeat the experiment. They were free to choose another number on which to place their colored counter. Most of the students moved their counters closer to the center of the chart.

After the second round of trials, Mr. Cuppett asked his students to tell which number they chose the first time around, which number they chose the second time around, and to give a reason why they switched. As students responded to the question, Mr. Cuppett kept tally marks of their answers. It was clear that something happened to change the students' choices. Most of the choices made in the first round were at the ends of the chart, but in the second round the students had decided to move to numbers such as 4, 5, 6, or 7. They weren't sure why this happened, but they learned that the extremes didn't have a lot of Xs above them.

The next question presented to the students was, "If two people were playing a game with two number cubes, and the rules said that player 1 could only move his playing piece if he rolled a 1, 2, 3, or 4 and player 2 could only move if she rolled a 5, 6, 7, or 8, who do you think would have a better chance of winning, and is this fair?" Hands immediately went up around the room: the overwhelming response was that, no, it wasn't fair.

The students still weren't sure why this was happening, so Mr. Cuppett asked them to take a close look at their cubes and tell him if it was possible to roll a total of 1 with two cubes. Even though a few thought this was possible, the majority quickly answered that this was not possible at all and that 2 was the smallest number you could roll because 1 was the smallest number on both cubes. He then asked them how they could make 2. Charlie knew right away that the only way to make a 2 was to roll two ones. The students were beginning to see that maybe the reason some of the other numbers came up more often on the cubes was because it was easier to roll those numbers. Charlie had certainly learned that it wasn't easy to roll two sixes. Each group set out to find the various ways to make the other sums using the cubes. Sarah found that you could make six by rolling a 1 and 5 or a 2 and 4 or a 3 and 3. Sean shared that he could make a 7 by rolling a 1 and 6 or a 2 and 5 or a 3 and 4. It was at this point that the students began to realize that certain sums would be found more often than others because there were more possible ways to make those numbers.

In this simulation, students were engaged in determining the combinations found by rolling two number cubes and finding the sum of those numbers. By getting actively involved, the students had an opportunity to construct some of their own meaning as they worked through the task. By making predictions, engaging in a meaningful simulation, and then comparing the results, the students had a chance to clarify their own thinking, and the teacher had a better picture of their understanding of the concept of fairness.

Conclusion

Representations are useful tools for supporting children's learning across all the mathematical strands. By learning how to show their thinking, students are developing skills that will serve them well as they progress into more advanced mathematics. We should support this growth by providing students with many opportunities to experience math in a tactile as well as a visual way, and by helping them to communicate their thinking through the use of manipulatives, pictures and diagrams, graphs, and numbers and symbols.

Questions for Discussion

1. In what ways can we connect the NCTM Content Standards with the Process Standards?

2. How can using manipulatives help students visualize a problem-solving situation?

3. Some teachers argue that using manipulatives slows down the instructional process. What arguments can you give to help change their thoughts?

4. Using a table in the cube problem helped students organize the data as they collected it. What are some other probability activities that our students would find interesting and that would encourage practice in using a table to organize data?

Accepting the Challenge

The Representation Standard

Principles and Standards for School Mathematics (NCTM 2000) describes representations as fundamental to understanding and applying mathematics. Representations give students a vehicle through which to process their thoughts, a mechanism to organize information, and an avenue for communicating about mathematics. The ways in which students use them give us, their teachers, insight into their level of understanding about various mathematical concepts, and they provide us with visual, hands-on ways in which to teach mathematics. In this book, we have discussed the importance of helping students learn to represent their mathematical thinking and ways in which they can do so. The very act of creating a representation of a concept helps to form an image of that knowledge in a student's mind and therefore a deeper understanding of that concept (Marzano et al. 2001). The goal of this book is to define what representations are, discuss the value in using them to explore mathematical topics, and illustrate how they might be used in a mathematics classroom. Through student work samples, examples of different representations, and activity suggestions, we hope to have made the case that the use of representations should be an integral component of any mathematics program.

Representations Support Learning

When students are learning to read, their teachers help them to develop a wide variety of strategies that will enable them to become confident, competent readers. Why should math be any different? Representation in math supports learning and helps students to develop a repertoire of strategies from which to select when faced with novel tasks. For example, students who know how to use blocks to represent equal groups, a repeating pattern, or the value of a number have models in their minds that they can reconstruct or simply visualize when attempting to solve a new or challenging problem. Students who are able to take a set of data and not only organize it into a

115

chart or graph but also interpret it in a way to make meaning of it have skills that they can use when faced with new or large amounts of information. Students who can generate a picture to show their understanding of a problem and then use the picture to help them solve the problem own a strategy that they can choose to use in many different situations. In addition, students who can apply numbers and symbols in a meaningful way to simple or complex mathematical processes are making connections between the concrete and abstract. Representations really support and show evidence of learning!

Manipulatives in Different Forms

Manipulatives come in many different forms, both concrete and virtual, and provide both students and teachers with a means to model different mathematical concepts and processes. How can we expect students to understand the value of numbers if they are exposed to the numbers only in digit form? It is through building and manipulating concrete numerical representations that students begin to get a sense of how both small and large numbers can really be and what the digits in a number stand for. Manipulatives provide us with concrete, visual benchmarks of certain mathematical concepts, on which we can draw later.

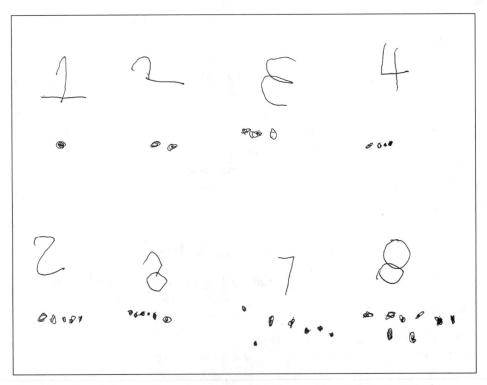

Representation helps students visualize models for problem solving in novel situations.

Virtual manipulatives offer students and teachers additional experiences in representing mathematical concepts. There isn't the threat of running out of blocks, and students can print an instant paper copy of their representation. In addition, although some older students might find it juvenile to use blocks, tiles, and other concrete manipulatives, they are excited about manipulating images of those blocks on the computer. An interactive white board provides a means for students to show their approach to solving a problem so all their peers can see it, which helps facilitate group discussion and strategizing. Technology is opening up a new world of possibilities for both teachers and students for exploring mathematical concepts.

We need to devote some time to thinking about which manipulatives we choose to use with our students because different manipulatives can result in students constructing different understandings. Students whose early math experiences are with base ten blocks, for example, are more likely to develop a units view of numbers (such as hundreds, tens, and ones), whereas students who have many experiences with tools associated with counting, such as hundreds charts or number lines, are more likely to see the counting aspects associated with solving certain problems. Careful consideration about the influence manipulatives may have on students' understandings is a necessary part of the planning process.

Pictures and Diagrams

Pictures and diagrams are useful tools for young mathematicians as they attempt to create meaning from mathematical situations. They are a natural next step after manipulatives as students progress from the concrete to the abstract. As students deal with more and more complex concepts and larger numbers, they may find it necessary to rely on alternate representations, such as pictures and diagrams, because concrete manipulatives may become too cumbersome. It is important to stress, however, that this progression from the concrete to the abstract should not occur until a child has a deep understanding of a mathematical concept and can communicate that understanding through concrete representations and words.

Pictures can give us great insight into a child's level of understanding about a concept. The ability to take the words from a math story or the numbers of a computation problem and create a visual representation in the form of a picture requires an understanding of the problem at hand. We can use the information we gain from studying children's pictorial representations to make instructional decisions that will meet their needs. Similarly, students can use the pictures or diagrams they create to help them communicate their thinking to others. It is oftentimes much easier for students to talk about pictures they have created to process a problem than it is to explain in words alone how they solved it. Working with our students to become proficient and efficient in creating pictorial representations should be one of our goals as we help to develop our students' mathematical abilities.

Diagrams, like pictures, provide students with another way to show understanding. Venn diagrams are extremely useful in helping organize students' thoughts about similarities and differences between two or more objects or concepts. We must be sure to include activities with graphic organizers such as Venn diagrams, flowcharts, and

T-charts to help students develop these comparison skills. Being able to compare and contrast requires high-level thinking at the analytical level, which leads to deeper understandings.

Numbers and Symbols

Just as students progress from concrete manipulatives to pictorial representations, they then progress to perhaps the most abstract form of representation: numbers and symbols. As students mature in their mathematical understandings, they reach a point where they are ready to learn about the numbers and symbols associated with concepts and processes. Timing is very important: introducing the abstract too early may result in shutting down the meaning- and sense-making processes in children, and they may become overly concerned with memorizing procedures and formulas rather than thinking about the mathematics involved in a situation. An important role of the teacher is to be attuned to each child's level of understanding at the concrete level *before* attempting to introduce numbers or symbols.

Once students have demonstrated a deep understanding of a mathematical concept, we have to be sure that students then develop a deep understanding of the numbers and symbols they will be using. It is absolutely essential that there is no confusion about what the equals sign means. We need to assess our students' understanding of this very basic and important element of an equation and clear up any misunderstandings that may exist. Without this fundamental knowledge, equations have little meaning to students, and as they progress in higher-level mathematics, the holes in their understandings will grow.

Invented algorithms are wonderful windows into a child's mind. Their unique ways of interpreting a problem and applying their own understandings to its solution provide us with a good idea of their level of understanding and whether there are any misconceptions. The invented procedures can also show us how students think about numbers. For example, when faced with a multidigit addition problem, if a child breaks up the numbers into units, finds partial sums, and then combines the parts to get a total, we can feel somewhat confident that the child has an understanding of place value and what the different steps in such a problem really mean. Information like this is invaluable as we plan experiences that will challenge our students and will also allow them to draw on their current understandings about different concepts.

Tables and Graphs

The purpose of graphing is to organize data in a meaningful display in order to make analysis of data easier. With this in mind, we need to plan meaningful experiences with graphing for our students. It is not enough to simply hand them a set of numbers and ask them to create a bar graph. Little understanding is developed through this passive approach to working with data. Rather, we need to think about graphing data with a purpose in mind: to answer a question that we or our students have posed and about which data have been collected. Once the data have been displayed on the appropriate type of graph, we must use the graph to answer the question originally posed.

Many of us spend too much time ensuring that our students know how to label a graph correctly and not enough time helping students to think about which graph would be most appropriate to display a set of data. Students need many experiences with different types of graphs so that they become familiar with their purposes and can make appropriate choices about which graph would be best for the task at hand. For example, students who choose to display the number of shoppers at a mall over an eight-hour period on a bar graph are not showing a deep understanding of the purpose of a bar graph or of the data. A line graph would be more appropriate for this type of data. Unless we give students many experiences creating and analyzing line graphs, they will probably not be able to correctly assign a line graph to a certain situation.

Most of the data displays with which students in prekindergarten through grade 2 become familiar are pictographs and bar graphs. They need to do more than just see them and hear about them, though; they need to create them using meaningful data and analyze them. Bulletin boards are wonderful ways to display large graphs of different types. They are visible to the whole class, and the graphs can be analyzed by the whole group, small groups, or by individuals. In the five minutes before lunch or dismissal, you can ask students to generate some true statements about the data on the graph. Two different graphs displayed side by side can serve as an opportunity to compare and contrast the two methods of displaying data and can serve as a discussion point about why each graph was chosen for the data it represents. Large visuals such as these can also allow for whole-group discussion about the shape of the data and about generalizations that can be made regarding the information displayed.

Graphing data is a wonderful tool for cross-curricular and multicultural activities and should be an integral part of our students' learning. With the vast resources available to us such as the Internet, newspapers, textbooks, and people around us, students have many opportunities to think about topics that interest them and to research those topics, collect data, and organize the data in an appropriate display. This active engagement in data analysis helps students to develop their critical and analytical skills with tasks that have meaning and are of interest to them.

Assessing Students' Representations

One of the more challenging aspects of a teacher's work is assessing student progress. Traditionally, the purpose of assessing students was to give teachers data in order to assign a grade. Fortunately, we use assessments for more meaningful purposes now, although we often still attach a grade to student performance. Assessment takes many forms, both formal and informal, and can be used to inform instruction, help students think about their learning, help parents understand their child's progress, and, most important, give us information about a child's level of understanding.

When faced with the task of assessing students' representations, we need to consider the purpose for which we are assessing. Is it to get a quick idea of whether a student understands a concept? Are we looking for mastery of a concept or skill? Are we looking for developmental growth in the use of representation? Depending on the desired outcome of the assessment, we have several options. We might simply listen in to a conversation between two students as they work together to solve a problem, making anecdotal notes as necessary. Or we might assign a performance-based assessment, asking students to represent a concept in a way that makes sense to them. We might also assign a task and collect paper copies of the representations the students did, analyzing them at a later time, perhaps using a rubric. Or we may just ask a student to explain what he is thinking about a particular problem. Each of these forms of assessment can help us as we plan meaningful mathematical experiences for our students.

How Classroom Teachers Can Make This Work

As teachers, we often have the most control over our students' immediate learning environment. We spend much time planning the layout of the room, the correct seating arrangement to ensure collaborative work, and the right displays for the walls to

The task this student is working on can be assessed in a variety of ways.

help the room seem inviting and comfortable for our students. In most classrooms a library is visible and accessible to students, but are math tools in a visible and accessible location too? Do we have number lines, graphics, and other mathematical representations hanging in our room to help support our students' learning in math similar to those for language arts? A wonderful compliment for us to receive as teachers is that we have as much numeracy visible in our room as we do literacy. We must strive to balance our efforts in all areas of the curriculum and to include as many mathematical displays as we do reading displays.

Having math tools in a visible and accessible location sends the message to our students and others that math is important and that we will use whatever tools are necessary to help students develop their mathematical thinking. Baskets of base ten blocks, linking cubes, counters, pattern blocks, rulers, string, markers, grid paper, and calculators, just to name a few, are some of the tools we want to provide for our students to use. Because math manipulatives can be expensive, one way to build up our classroom supply is to solicit material from our students' parents and our colleagues. Many items commonly found in our homes can serve as math manipulatives, such as coins, beans, toothpicks, craft sticks, ribbon, and containers, and parents are usually more than happy to help out by sending them in. We just have to ask!

One of the most important ways in which we can help to develop our students into competent and confident mathematicians is to become competent and confident mathematicians ourselves. It is not enough to rely on the math we learned in elementary school. A quick survey of our colleagues will likely show that the way they learned math was not a process of concept development and understanding but a process of memorizing algorithms and procedures and doing as they were told. Fortunately, that approach to mathematics instruction is no longer the norm. However, that places a new challenge on us to develop a deep understanding of the mathematical concepts we experienced only superficially when we were in school. Community colleges, local universities, and district-provided professional development offer ways in which we can relearn the math that we will be teaching our students. Without this strong content knowledge, it is difficult to analyze our students' representations to determine their level of understanding about a concept and then to determine the next steps to further their growth. It is only through having a deep understanding of the mathematics ourselves that we will be able to anticipate misconceptions by our students and to push our students to think more deeply about mathematics.

How School Administrators Can Make This Work

Classroom teachers have the most direct impact on students' learning, but school administrators can support teachers in many ways in this task. First, they can allocate funds to purchase high-quality math materials, such as base ten blocks, pattern blocks, geometric solids, fraction circles or squares, tiles, geoboards, and Cuisenaire rods, as well as invest in technology that will support student representations, such as software and interactive white boards. It would be wonderful if there were a set of manipulatives in each room, but at the minimum there should be one set for every two classrooms to share. Second, administrators can work with teachers and specialists to set up the master schedule so that team members have time to collaborate and talk about the mathematics they are teaching, and to actually experience concepts and activities *before* introducing them to the students. This is one of the best means for anticipating student misconceptions and planning appropriate responses to them. Finally, administrators can support professional development that will enhance their teachers' math content knowledge. This can be done by paying for teachers to attend math content classes, inviting a math consultant to come to the school, and purchasing teacher resources such as books and materials. School administrators are the instructional leaders in the school. By modeling a learning spirit, they encourage their teachers to further develop themselves.

Another way in which administrators can help students deepen their mathematical understandings through representations is by displaying representations around the school. With the help of the student council association, they can conduct a survey of students to learn about their suggestions for spirit days throughout the year. The data can be compiled into a graphical display that can be posted in the main hall (or outside the gymnasium, where there always seems to be some downtime!) or in some other central location where children will be able to see it, think about it, and discuss it. Another suggestion is to work with the school librarian to display information about types of books checked out by grade level. Again, student representatives could help in creating the data display. Aside from graphical representations, administrators can support the display of visual representations around the school by encouraging classroom teachers to hang student-generated examples from completed class activities, such as Venn diagrams or representations of sorted polygons, outside their rooms. By communicating the message through words and actions that mathematical learning is important and valued, administrators can support teacher efforts to develop competent, confident mathematicians.

The Challenge to Teachers

We are entering a new and exciting era of teaching and learning mathematics, one that challenges students to explore, struggle with, and create their own understandings of mathematical concepts. Students are no longer handed knowledge through formulas or algorithms, but instead develop their own knowledge as a result of firsthand experiences. To meet this challenge, we must be willing to rethink the way we approach mathematics instruction. We must begin to view ourselves as experts in the content we teach, and as such, we need to do whatever it takes to become an expert: take a math content course, engage in regular dialogue with our colleagues about the math we teach, attend professional development seminars, and so on. To be able to help our students think deeply about the mathematics they are learning, we must also think deeply about it.

The use of representations provides a particularly exciting opportunity to begin to think in more depth about math content. How will we use manipulatives to get children to think about the magnitude of a number? How will we show in pictorial form the meaning of a math story? In what ways can we use numbers and symbols to synthesize our thinking? These are questions we must ask ourselves at the same time that we are asking our students to represent their thinking. It is a wonderful, exciting time to be a math teacher, and to meet the challenge of preparing our students to become confident, competent mathematicians, we must also become the same.

Questions for Discussion

1. What are the most important pieces of knowledge you have gained from reading this book?

2. What are ways in which teachers can support an environment that values mathematical representations?

3. What are ways in which administrators can support an environment that values mathematical representations?

4. How will you change aspects of your instructional planning to ensure that you give deep thought to the mathematics before introducing it to students?

The following resources are meant to support you as you continue to explore the representation standard in prekindergarten through grade 2. You will find a variety of text resources—books that provide additional activities and instructional strategies that encourage student representations. A list of math-related literature books and math websites are included to supply you with classroom tasks, electronic manipulative ideas, and teacher resources.

Text Resources

The following text resources provide a variety of activities and strategies for supporting students as they develop their skills in representing mathematical thinking.

Abrohms, A. 1992. *Problem Solving with Pentominoes: Grades 1–4 Activity Book*. Lincolnshire, IL: Learning Resources.

Andrini, B. 1991. *Cooperative Learning and Mathematics*. San Juan Capistrano, CA: Resources for Teachers.

Bender, W. 2005. *Differentiating Math Instruction: Strategies That Work for K–8 Classrooms*. Thousand Oaks, CA: Sage.

Bosse, N. R. 1995. *Writing Mathematics*. Chicago: Creative Publications.

Burns, M. 1992. *The Way to Math Solutions*. Sausalito, CA: Math Solutions.

———. 1996. *50 Problem Solving Lessons, Grades 1–6*. Sausalito, CA: Math Solutions.

———. 2002. *About Teaching Mathematics*. Sausalito, CA: Math Solutions.

Charles, L. H. 1990. *Algebra Thinking: First Experiences*. Chicago: McGraw Hill/Wright Group.

Countryman, J. 1992. *Writing to Learn Mathematics*. Portsmouth, NH: Heinemann.

Dacey, L., and R. Eston. 2002. *Show and Tell: Representing and Communicating Mathematical Ideas in K–2 Classrooms*. Sausalito, CA: Math Solutions.

Greenes, C., and C. Findell. 1999. *Groundworks: Algebraic Thinking, Grade 2*. Chicago: Creative Publications.

Hersch, S., A. Cameron, M. Dolk, and C. Twomey Fosnot. 2004. *Fostering Children's Mathematical Development, Grades PreK–3*. Portsmouth, NH: Heinemann.

Jones, G. A., and C. A. Thornton. 1992. *Data, Chance & Probability: Grades 1–3 Activity Book.* Vernon Hills, IL: Learning Resources.

Kagan, S. 1992. *Cooperative Learning.* San Clemente, CA: Resources for Teachers.

McIntosh, M., and R. J. Draper. 1997. *Write Starts.* New York: Dale Seymour.

Miller, E. 2001. *Read It! Draw It! Solve It!* Parsippany, NJ: Dale Seymour.

National Council of Teachers of Mathematics. 2001. *Navigating Through Geometry in Prekindergarten–Grade 2.* Reston, VA: Author.

Newman, V. 1994. *Math Journals.* San Diego: Teaching Resource Center.

O'Connell, S. 1997. *Glyphs! Data Communication for Primary Mathematicians.* Columbus, OH: Frank Schaffer.

———. 2001. *Math—The Write Way for Grades 2–3.* Columbus, OH: Frank Schaffer.

———. 2005. *Now I Get It: Strategies for Building Confident and Competent Mathematicians K–6.* Portsmouth, NH: Heinemann.

Richardson, K. 1999. *Developing Number Concepts.* White Plains, NY: Dale Seymour.

Stewart, K., K. Walker, and C. Reak. 1995. *Thinking Questions for Pattern Blocks, Grades 1–3.* Chicago: Creative Publications.

Van de Walle, J. A., and L. H. Lovin. 2006. *Teaching Student-Centered Mathematics, Grades K–3.* New York: Pearson Education.

Whitin, P., and D. Whitin. 2000. *Math Is Language Too: Talking and Writing in the Mathematics Classroom.* Urbana, IL: National Council of Teachers of English.

———. 2003. *A Mathematical Passage: Strategies for Promoting Inquiry in Grades 4–6.* Portsmouth, NH: Heinemann.

Zikes, D. 2003. *Big Book of Math K–6.* San Antonio: Dinah-Might Adventures.

Math-Literature Connections

One of the ways teachers can help students learn how to represent their mathematical thinking is by using literature books to anchor an activity or lesson. There are an increasing number of books on the market today designed to link math and reading.

Adler, D. 1998. *Shape Up! Fun with Triangles and Other Polygons.* New York: Holiday House.

Anno, M. 1983. *Anno's Magic Seeds.* New York: Putnam.

———. 1983. *Anno's Mysterious Multiplying Jar.* New York: Philomel.

Axelrod, A. 2000. *Pigs at Odds.* New York: Simon and Schuster.

Barrett, J. 1978. *Cloudy with a Chance of Meatballs.* New York: Aladdin.

Burns, M. 1994. *The Greedy Triangle.* New York: Scholastic.

———. 1997. *Spaghetti and Meatballs for All! A Mathematical Story.* New York: Scholastic.

Caple, K. 1985. *The Biggest Nose.* Boston: Houghton Mifflin.

Cushman, J. 1991. *Do You Wanna Bet?* New York: Clarion Books.

Dahl, R. 1982. *The BFG.* New York: Puffin.

Hutchins, P. 1986. *The Doorbell Rang.* New York: Mulberry.

Gold, K. 1998. *Numbers Every Day.* New York. Newbridge Educational.

Lasky, K. 1994. *The Librarian Who Measured the Earth.* Boston: Little, Brown.

Neuschwander, C. 1997. *Sir Cumference and the First Round Table: A Math Adventure.* Watertown, MA: Charlesbridge.

———. 1998. *Amanda Bean's Amazing Dream: A Mathematical Story.* New York: Scholastic.

Pallotta, J. 1999. *Hershey's Fraction Book. Hershey's Food.* New York: Scholastic.

Pollack, P., and M. Belviso. 2002. *Chickens on the Move.* New York: Kane.

Schlein, M. 1996. *More Than One.* New York: Greenwillow.

Schwartz, D. 1997. *How Much Is a Million?* New York: Mulberry.

———. 1999. *On Beyond a Million*. New York: Random House.
Scieszka, J., and L. Smith. 1995. *Math Curse*. New York: Viking.
Silverstein, S. 1974. *Where the Sidewalk Ends*. New York: HarperCollins.

Websites

The following websites provide ideas and activities to use with students in helping them represent their math thinking.

www.k111.k12.il.us/king/math.htm—This website has lots of interactive activities for the primary grades. Many of the activities require the Shockwave plug-in.

http://illuminations.nctm.org/lessonplans/prek-2/dominoes/index.html#l1— This instructional unit focuses on addition for students who have learned to count but have not yet mastered addition of one-digit numbers. These lessons also explore foundational algebraic understandings.

www.aaamath.com—This site contains interactive games and lesson plans.

www.glc.k12.ga.us/BuilderV03/lptools/lpshared/lpdisplay.asp?Session_Stamp= &LPID=13142—A hands-on lesson that includes a PowerPoint presentation in which students use length to order objects from longest to shortest.

www.glc.k12.ga.us/BuilderV03/lptools/lpshared/lpdisplay.asp?Session_Stamp= &LPID=15678—A lesson plan that compares students' heights (taller/shorter) and compares lengths of straws (longer/shorter).

www.sbgmath.com/grk/chapter7/start/index.html—A pennies activity with Internet links to information about American coins.

www.glc.k12.ga.us/BuilderV03/lptools/lpshared/lpdisplay.asp?Session_Stamp= &LPID=13293—A hands-on lesson in which students sort geometric figures by color, size, and shape.

http://ericir.syr.edu/cgi-bin/printlessons.cgi/Virtual/Lessons/Mathematics/ Process_Skills/MPS0004.html—A lesson plan describing graphing and sorting activities with jelly beans.

Rubrics

There are several great websites for making rubrics or using ready-made rubrics.

http://rubistar.4teachers.org/index.php
www.teach-nology.com/web_tools/rubrics/
www.teachervision.fen.com/teaching-methods/rubrics/4521.html
www.education-world.com/a_curr/curr248.shtml

Other Resources

www.nctm.org—The National Council of Teachers of Mathematics website
www.mathcats.com/explore/polygons.html

Burns, M. 2002. *About Teaching Mathematics.* Sausalito, CA: Math Solutions.

Fisher, S., and C. Hartmann. 2005. "Math through the Mind's Eye." *Mathematics Teacher* 99 (4): 246–250.

Hiebert, J., T. Carpenter, E. Fennema, K. Fuson, D. Wearne, H. Murray, A. Olivier, and P. Human. 1997. *Making Sense.* Portsmouth, NH: Heinemann.

Hiebert, J., R. Gallimore, H. Garnier, K. Bogard Givvin, H. Hollingsworth, J. Jacobs, A. Miu-Ying Chui, D. Wearne, M. Smith, N. Kersting, A. Manaster, E. Tseng, W. Etterbeek, C. Manaster, P. Gonzales, and J. Stigler. 2003. *Teaching Mathematics in Seven Countries: Results from the TIMSS 1999 Video Study* (NCES 2003–013 Revised). Washington, DC: U.S. Department of Education, National Center for Education Statistics.

Marzano, R., D. Pickering, and J. Pollock. 2001. *Classroom Instruction that Works.* Alexandria, VA: Association for Supervision and Curriculum Development.

Moyer, P., J. Bolyard, and M. Spikell. 2002. "What Are Virtual Manipulatives?" *Teaching Children Mathematics.* Reston, VA: National Council of Teachers of Mathematics.

National Council of Teachers of Mathematics. 1989. *Curriculum and Evaluation Standards for School Mathematics.* Reston, VA: Author.

———. 2000. *Principles and Standards for School Mathematics.* Reston, VA: Author.

Nolan, H. 2001. *How Much, How Many, How Far, How Heavy, How Long, How Tall Is 1,000?* Toronto: Kids Can Press.

Pallotta, J. 2003. *Count to a Million.* New York: Scholastic.

Schwartz, D. 1993. *How Much Is a Million?* New York: Mulberry Books.

Why Are the Activities on a CD?

At first glance, the CD included with this book appears to be a collection of teaching tools and student activities, much like the activities that appear in many teacher resource books. But instead of taking a book to the copier to copy an activity, with the CD you can simply print off the desired page on your home or work computer. No more standing in line at the copier or struggling to carefully position the book on the copier so you can make a clean copy. And with our busy schedules, we appreciate having activities that are classroom ready and aligned with our math standards.

You may want to simplify some tasks or add complexity to others. The problems on the CD often include several parts or have added challenge extensions. When it is appropriate for your students, simply delete these sections for a quick way to simplify or shorten the tasks.

Editing the CD to Motivate and Engage Students

Personalizing Tasks or Capitalizing on Students' Interests

The editable CD provides a quick and easy way to personalize math problems. Substituting students' names, the teacher's name, or a favorite restaurant, sports team, or location can immediately engage students.

Name _____

Sports Night

Second-grade students completed a survey of the after-school sports they played. According to the survey, a total of 14 students played basketball, and 16 students played soccer. If the rest of the 50 students surveyed played baseball, how many students played baseball? Complete the tally chart below to show your answer.

Sport	
Basketball	Ոℍ Ոℍ IIII
Soccer	ℍ ℍ ℍ I
Baseball	

Modifying the Readability of Tasks

Adding some fun details can generate interest and excitement in story problems, but you might prefer to modify some problems for students with limited reading ability. Simply deleting some of the words on the editable CD will result in an easy-to-read version of the same task, as shown in the second version of the following problem.

Name _____

Spilled Coins

Oops! Carly spilled some coins out of her piggy bank. 5 coins fell out that total 27¢. What coins fell out of her bank?

Show your thinking.

Name _____

Spilled Coins

5 coins spilled out of a bank. They total 27¢. What coins fell out of her bank?

Show your thinking.

Creating Shortened or Tiered Tasks

Although many students are able to move from one task to another, some students benefit from focusing on one task at a time. By simply separating parts of a task, either by cutting the page into sections or by using the editable CD feature to put the parts of the task on separate pages, teachers can help focus students on the first part of the task before moving them on to the next part.

Name _____

What numbers fit in each shape? Same shapes are the same number.

◯ + ◯ = 12   ▢ + ◯ = 10

What number is ◯ ?_____

What number is ▢ ?_____

How did you figure out what numbers fit?

_____

_____

_____

_____

_____

_____

_____

_____

Name _____

What numbers fit in each shape? Same shapes are the same number.

◯ + ◯ = 12

What number is ◯ ?_____

How do you know?

_____

_____

_____

▢ + ◯ = 10

What number is ▢ ?_____

How do you know?

_____

_____

Modifying Data

While all students may work on the same problem task, modifying the problem data allows teachers to create varying versions of the task. Using the editable CD, you can either simplify the data or insert more challenging data including larger numbers, monetary amounts, or fractions.

Name _____

I Went to the Store (1)

I went to the store and bought a banana that cost 40¢. I gave the clerk $1.00. How much change did I get back?

Show your thinking.

Name _____

I Went to the Store (2)

I went to the store and bought a bunch of bananas that cost $1.89. I gave the clerk $5.00. How much change did I get back?

Show your thinking.

The editable CD allows you to quickly change the level of cognitive demand a task requires. This simple change may relieve anxiety for many students. Version 2 still presents a challenging task, but it may be more doable for some students within your class.

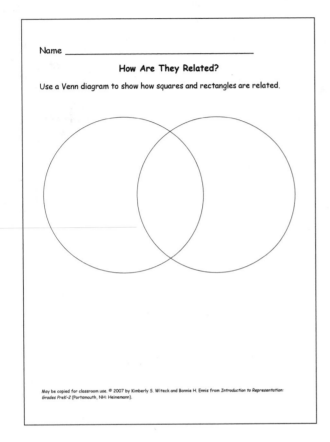

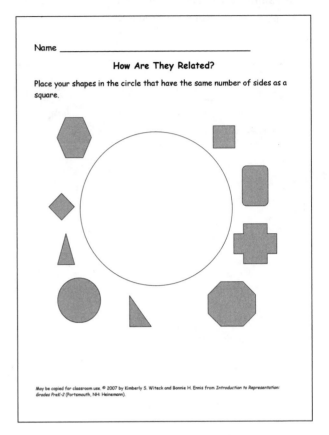

Some of the problem tasks on the CD include challenge questions at the bottom of the page. These tasks provide a way to extend the task, but they can be deleted easily if you feel students have neither the time nor the ability to complete the tasks. In version 2 of the next example, the challenge task was deleted.

Name _____

Spaghetti and Change

Suppose you bought a package of spaghetti and a jar of sauce for $3.62 and gave the clerk $5.00. How much change should you get back?

Show your thinking.

Challenge: What bills and coins would you get back if you want the fewest coins possible? _____

_____

_____

_____

Name _____

Spaghetti and Change

Suppose you bought a package of spaghetti and a jar of sauce for $3.62 and gave the clerk $5.00. How much change should you get back?

Show your thinking.